Who We Were, What We Did

Fresh Perspectives on Grand Traverse History

© 2009 Richard Fidler. All rights reserved. No portion of this book may be reproduced in any form, electronic or mechanical, without the written permission of the Traverse Area Historical Society Board of Directors except for brief excerpts in media reviews.

Traverse Area Historical Society
322 Sixth Street
Traverse City, MI 49684
231-929-7663

For information, please contact Richard Fidler at rafidler@sbcglobal.net

ISBN 978-0-9761027-4-8

Printed and bound in the United States
First printing 2009

Cover and book design by Saxon Design, Inc., Traverse City, MI

Who We Were, What We Did

Fresh Perspectives on Grand Traverse History

Richard Fidler

To Chris, Lauren, Harry
Richard Fidler

TRAVERSE AREA HISTORICAL SOCIETY
TRAVERSE CITY, MICHIGAN

To the Veterans of the
Spanish-American War
and World War I
who stood up,
And to Thomas H. Coxe,
who did not

Contents

ACKNOWLEDGEMENTS	ix
INTRODUCTION	xi
CHAPTER 1 • The First Portrait of Traverse City *A Look at an 1873 Lithograph of the Traverse Area*	1
CHAPTER 2 • Listening to Dissonant Voices *Dissent in Traverse City during the First World War*	5
CHAPTER 3 • Celebrating the Fourth in Northwestern Michigan *A Historical Remembrance*	13
CHAPTER 4 • From Doctor's Visits to the Modern Hospital *How Medical Care has Changed in the Traverse Area*	21
CHAPTER 5 • Of Vagrants, Poor Funds, and Poor Houses *Poverty a Hundred Years Ago*	31
CHAPTER 6 • The Veterans Memorial Highway *Rediscovering Living Monuments to Spanish-American and World War I Soldiers*	39
CHAPTER 7 • Crime and Justice A Century Ago *Examining the Jail Record of Grand Traverse County*	45

CHAPTER 8 • Where Is the Park on Park Street?
A Study of Traverse City Street Names — 55

CHAPTER 9 • Of Obedience, Truthfulness, and Self-Control
Dr. James Decker Munson's Views on Preventing Insanity — 61

CHAPTER 10 • "Many Wonderful Transitions"
Changes in the Treatment of Mental Illness, 1885-1910 — 71

CHAPTER 11 • What Do Old Textbooks Tell Us of the Past?
The Values Taught at School a Hundred Years Ago — 81

CHAPTER 12 • How We Changed the Lake
Tracing the Impacts of Settlement on Grand Traverse Bay and Lake Michigan — 91

CHAPTER 13 • How We Changed the Land
Tracing the Impacts of Settlement on the Forests of Northern Michigan — 101

CHAPTER 14 • Life at the End of a Peninsula
How Geography Shapes our Community — 109

CHAPTER 15 • "Say, Sis, Is the Doctor In?"
The Life of Augusta Louise Rosenthal Thompson, M.D — 117

    Introduction
    Life of Augusta Louise Rosenthal-Thompson
    Timeline showing important events in Dr. Rosenthal-Thompson's life

SOURCES — 127

Acknowledgements

A book is a product of the efforts of many. Marlas Hanson, reference librarian of the Traverse Area District Library, has been greatly helpful in locating references and in pointing out leads for new stories. Thanks go to biologists David Clapp and Ned Fogle for providing critical comment on "How We Changed the Lake." The Traverse Area Historical Society was generous in sharing its collection of historical photographs. The Archives of Michigan was helpful in granting access to the *Jail Record Book of Grand Traverse County*. I am grateful to my wife Sharon and to Kathie McDonald who took on the onerous duty of proofreading and editing this book. However much effort has gone into cleaning it up, the imperfections ultimately belong to me.

The Grand Traverse Herald building, Front Street, late 19th century. (Traverse Area Historical Society)

Introduction

This book is made up of a diverse collection of written pieces. They are diverse in their content—subjects range from the first pictorial representation of Traverse City to the climate of dissent during the First World War—and they are diverse in tone and language with some pieces to be enjoyed as an easy read before bed and others to be studied with more care. While at first I had concerns about the work's unity, in the end I trusted the reader's instinct to attempt new things.

Most of these pieces begin with a question: A hundred years ago, who took care of the poor? Who occupied the jail and what were they arrested for? Was there any opposition to the Great War locally? What was the Bay like before settlement and how did it change? An artifact from the past might provoke the discussion: an old school textbook, an antique map, a forgotten newspaper article preserved on microfilm. After examining them, I found the hard part came in thinking about their meaning: What social values are implied? Did everyone accept them? Do we hold those values today? If not, how did they change? Such questions make history an exploration of our humanity. That is what makes the subject interesting to me.

I deliberated for a long time before choosing the title *Who We Were, What We Did: Fresh Perspectives on Grand Traverse History*. It was necessary to tell potential readers this was not only a book of history, but also a book of reflections from a point of view not commonly entertained by local writers. Like my previous book, *Glimpses of Grand Traverse Past*, it takes on controversial topics: racism, dissent, attitudes towards the poor, and the pillaging of the natural world. These stories of our past need to be told. Our history is incomplete without them.

The last piece is not about historical inquiry. It is a simple biography of an extraordinary doctor who practiced in Traverse City a long time ago. Originally, I hoped it might be printed as a short book in its own right, but that proved not feasible. Consequently, I present it to readers together with a short introduction and a timeline chronicling the events in the life of Augusta Louise Rosenthal-Thompson. She was a luminary person who deserves to be remembered in this community.

Richard Fidler
April, 2009

TRAVERSE CITY AND ITS PIONEERS.

1873 view of the Traverse area (Traverse Area Historical Society)

CHAPTER 1

The First Portrait of Traverse City
A Look at an 1873 Lithograph of the Traverse Area

The first true representation of Traverse City was less a map and more a work of art.[1] At its creation in 1873, it advertised the Northern Michigan way of life with its renderings of sailboats, fishing gear, cross-cut saws and peaveys, hunting rifles, and a peaceful Indian village. At the four corners of the picture, (perhaps because the work may have been commissioned by them), four early settlers are honored with cameo portraits: Perry Hannah, Morgan Bates, David C. Goodale, and Cuyler Germaine.[2] A vocational symbol underlies each one: businessman Hannah with a factory ledger book, editor Bates with a rolled newspaper, Dr. Goodale with a bottle of calomine medicine, and lumberman Germaine with something that might be a handle of a logging cant. Unsmiling, they peer at us with nineteenth century gravity.

The view of Traverse City is from Old Mission peninsula, looking south towards the town on West Bay. Few structures are visible from this vantage point, but omitting them could have been a good artistic and practical decision since images of dusty or muddy roads and shabby frame buildings would not encourage immigrants to come and stay. It is better to focus on the beauty of Nature. However, in a nod to prospective farm-

Dandelion illustration by William Holdsworth from *Lessons with Plants* by L.H. Bailey

ers, a plow, a basket of apples, pumpkins, ears of corn, and piles of vegetables and fruit are laid out for all to see. The lesson is clear: the Grand Traverse area is a fine place to plant an orchard or sow a field!

The young settlement was not completely isolated, since a curve of railroad track bends around the foot of the bay in an inset view at the bottom of the picture. Railroads were often featured in early promotional maps and artwork. They pointed to easy access to larger centers of population and low cost freight delivery. By 1873 the tracks had reached Traverse City, the construction costs having been borne by Hannah and others.[3] Now that the investment had been made, it was time to use the railroad asset to bring settlers to the region. That is why the picture of the railroad occupies a central position in the work: it promises further population growth in this place so separated by geography from the east-west traffic across the nation.

Who created this first view of Traverse City? At the bottom we can read "Designed and Drawn on Stone by Willie Holdsworth." A local boy, William Holdsworth was no more than eighteen years old at the time he made this lithograph.[4] He went on

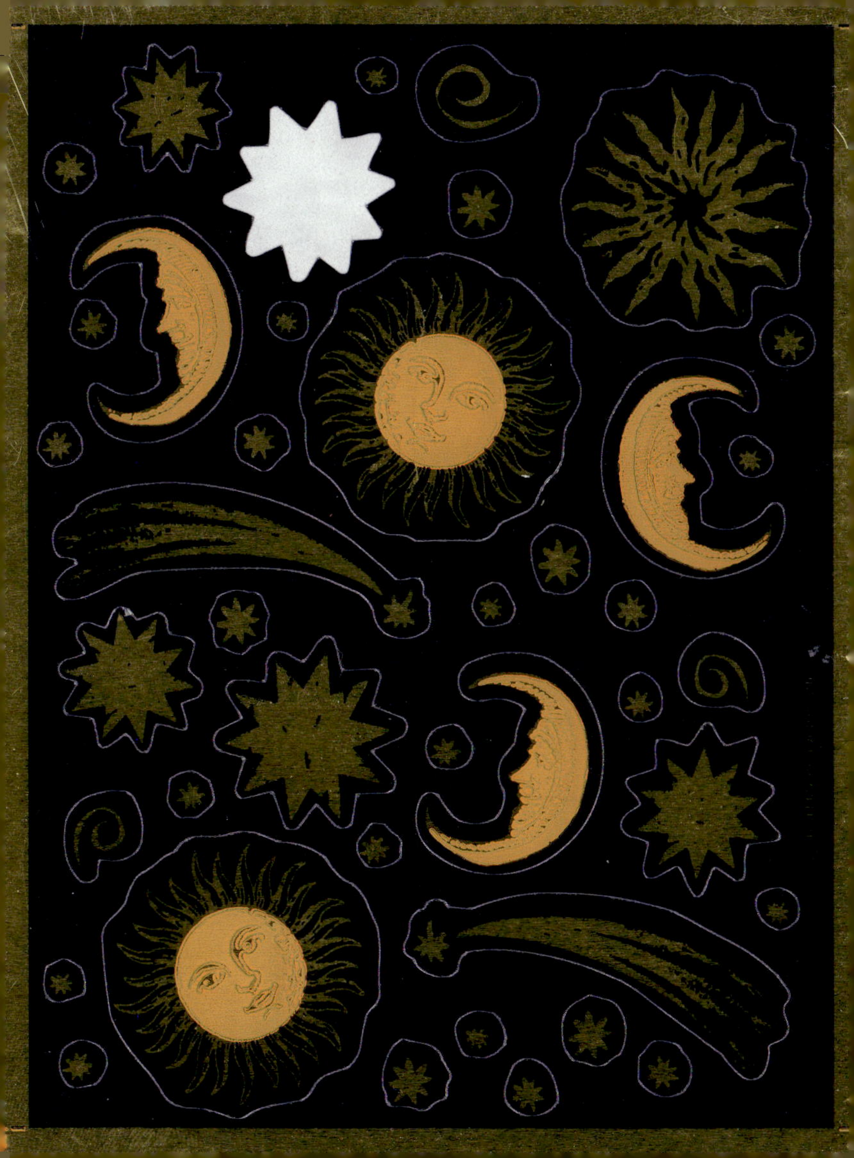

to graduate from the Michigan Agricultural College in 1878, eventually joining the art faculty at that school. Late in his career, he was chosen to illustrate L.H. Bailey's botany text, *Lessons with Plants*. The diagrams and drawings presented there go far beyond basic biological illustration; they display the skillful expression of a master draftsman and artist. Unfortunately, he died of consumption at the relatively young age of 53, before his reputation had a chance to flower.

Trailing arbutus illustration by William Holdsworth from *Lessons with Plants* by L.H. Bailey

Traverse City has been portrayed in various ways over the course of its history. At first, in accordance with state law, it was shown on an 1852 plat map, a pen-and-ink effort that named the streets around the courthouse and delineated individual lots and public places. In 1879 the Traverse City panoramic map—also called a bird's eye view—was commissioned. A combination of cartography and artistry, it showed the Bay, the streets, frame buildings, trees and hills. Finally, the Sanborn Fire Insurance map of 1929 colorfully displays blocks, schools, churches, and public buildings from overhead, concentric circles telling how far places are from the courthouse. Of them all, the 1873 Holdsworth representation is the most dear. It alone captures the spirit of Grand Traverse during the first years of settlement, picturing trees, hills and water as well as Native Americans and early pioneers. As we view it across the gap of one-hundred thirty-five years, we can see things that still resonate with us: the contours of the land, the curve of the Bay, the omnipresence of Nature. Truly, even now it speaks to us of home.

CHAPTER 2
Listening to Dissonant Voices
Dissent in Traverse City during the First World War

The peculiar evil of silencing the expression of an opinion is, that it is robbing the human race; posterity as well as the existing generation; those who dissent from the opinion, still more than those who hold it. If the opinion is right, they are deprived of the opportunity of exchanging error for truth: if wrong, they lose, what is almost as great a benefit, the clearer perception and livelier impression of truth, produced by its collision with error.
–John Stuart Mill, philosopher and economist (1806-1873)

      In early 1917 the world was aflame with war. Europe was engulfed with the fire; German tanks and artillery spread over the landscape and German U-Boats patrolled the seas. In the United States, Hearst and other newspapers clamored for the entrance of the United States into the conflict and achieved success in their quest. The United States entered the war on April 6, 1917.

It was a time of great patriotism and unrest. Locally, the Elk Rapids school district resolved to stop teaching German since doing so only promoted the hateful culture of the Huns. With the Michigan National Guard being sent to Germany, Traverse City created its own fighting force, a branch of the Michigan Home Guard, to protect local property from possible destruction by German sympathizers. One man of the group stated:

> Traverse City had enough deer hunters who could still use a rifle to form a company of men who could protect property at home or any other place to which they might be sent.

A local drunk, Karl Temple, was arrested for saying he supported the German side and was imprisoned as a danger to America. Liberty Bonds were sold to pay for the war and those unwilling to purchase them were labeled shirkers. Patriotic fifth graders at Union Street School in Traverse City refused to sing the German song, "Watch on the Rhine." Downstate, a woman was tarred and feathered as a German sympathizer while her husband, bound to a chair, was forced to watch. Things got so bad that the Michigan Governor, Albert Sleeper, issued a proclamation decrying vigilante action on the part of mobs aroused by hatred for all things German.

At this difficult time in American history, was there national opposition to a war that provoked such patriotic feeling? Beyond that, were there local figures who spoke out against social injustice and pro-war public sentiment? Dissent at this time was dangerous. Besides the possibilities of beatings and social ostracism, there was the very real possibility of being arrested for opposing the war. Congress passed the Espionage Act of 1917, a measure which made it a crime to speak out forcefully against the war. Publishing antiwar views could be a federal offense.

Nationally, Progressive Robert LaFollette of Wisconsin resisted the call to war. Speaking in Congress, he attempted to halt the movement towards joining the conflict. For his efforts he faced an angry response from the Senate and from most Americans. Austin Batdorff, editor of the *Record-Eagle* at this time, expressed the opinion of most of his paper's readership:

> The hour of the pacifist, the mollycoddle statesman and the pro-German American, has passed; from today on, every true American will bury his beliefs, his fears, his biases in his patriotic love of country, his convictions for democratic government and his determination that, right or wrong, this nation must defend itself against an enemy that has been given every opportunity to avert war and which has replied with insolence, insult and wanton destruction of American lives.

Upon formal declaration of war, the pacifist movement lost the power to influence public opinion: Opposition to the war became suspect, unwelcome if not traitorous. Batdorff wrote:

> When [the president] speaks we either must obey like patriotic soldiers or refuse to obey like disloyal renegades.

Courage was called for in questioning the decision to go to war.

Opposition to the war came from two centers: religious pacifists and socialists who saw it as a way of exploiting workingmen. Locally there is no evidence that religious pacifists—such as the Society of Friends—protested conscription or the war. There was a socialist presence in Traverse City that, like most socialists nation-wide, resisted the involvement of the United States in the war. Though small in numbers (locally about 8% of the 1916 vote for president went to the socialist candidate, Eugene V. Debs), the group was large enough to support a weekly newspaper, *Honest Opinion*, which circulated for a year or two—history is not clear on the dates of its founding or demise. In fact, only a few issues survive on microfilm.

Perhaps the idea of socialists in a Northern Michigan small town with such a long-standing conservative legacy would surprise many readers. At this time, Traverse City was an industrial city. It did not survive solely by the cherry industry and summer resorts, but had a large and varied industrial base. The Oval Wood Dish Company had operated here for many years, and cigar factories, the Amniotte candy factory, and the canning factory employed many hundreds of workers, both men and women. In general they were much underpaid even by standards of the time. The *Traverse City Record-*

Eagle did not represent their interests, showcasing the views of wealthy businessmen in town instead. Against the economic power of that paper, *Honest Opinion* could persist upon the streets of the city for only a short time. Even so, the few thin copies that remain provide us with a window into the lives of working men and women who struggled to survive in a difficult environment.

One of the copies issued on Memorial Day, May, 29, 1919, tiptoes carefully in raising questions about the justice of the recent war. The editor wrote:

> Again let us bow our heads in honor and in memory of these brave men for whom this day has been set apart and if there be any bitterness let it be directed at those who made wars and words but have never fought them. We have no fight with the soldier though we may have with those who teach him and our reverence today does and should go forth to him never to be forgotten while the words of the orator who was at home will pass from our minds as does a drifting perfume on a breath of wind.

An early portrait of Thomas H. Coxe, editor of *Honest Opinion*
(Traverse Area Historical Society)

The idea that veterans are to receive honor for their service even if high officials have not always acted honorably resonates today after the legality and morality of recent wars have been questioned. It is a humane thought, spoken by a veteran, Thomas Coxe, who had fought in the Spanish-American War.

Coxe had a reputation in Traverse City. In 1917 he refused to stand during the playing of the "Star Spangled Banner" at a city commission meeting in which the sale of liberty bonds was discussed. In fact, three times the anthem was played, and three times he refused to stand. For his efforts, he was beaten by the enraged crowd. Upon being contacted by the *Record-Eagle* the next day, he gave this statement:

I am a firm believer in democracy and served my country in the Spanish-American war because I believe that the Star Spangled Banner in principle, stands for honesty, justice, equality, free speech, free press, freedom and liberty. I am against using the Star Spangled Banner for advertising purposes or the purpose of coercing public officials to vote against their conscience and what they believe is right.

※

Honest Opinion had a predecessor in town. Though not socialist, the *Traverse City Press* promised to present the views of all citizens. In an alliance with the Chamber of Commerce it advocated Open Forums, public discussions on a variety of issues, both local and national. Harold Titus, later to become a well-known novelist, championed the forums and several were enacted at the City Opera House. One was devoted to the inadequate salaries of Traverse City teachers, with Julius Steinberg, a powerful businessman, taking the position that the teachers were underpaid. Several persons spoke out in opposition, including the superintendent of schools. Perhaps the uproar thereby created explains why the Forums were soon discontinued. In the end, free discussion of sensitive issues was not as welcome as organizers had supposed.

The *Traverse City Press* soon degenerated into little more than an advertising circular with jokes, gossip, and fluff filling its pages. At first, however, when its editor was the same Thomas Coxe who later edited *Honest Opinion*, the Press dared to publish letters from its working class readers that described life from a perspective not available in the *Traverse City Record-Eagle*. One woman wrote in February, 1917:

> Right about face, Traverse City and see yourself as others see you. In your *City Press* of last week was an article stating as an inducement for factories to locate "among us," it was a fact your manufacturers were paying an average wage of 470 dollars per year.

> Statistics tell us that it requires an average wage of 800 dollars per year to keep the average family in just an existing condition. The fact remains that your laboring men's family are living on half of what it takes to keep an average family. That means that they must depend on charity for the balance or go without. The appearance of most of your people on your streets are doing both.

The writer went on to say how the Chamber of Commerce had induced manufacturers to move to Traverse City playing up the cheap women's labor force.

> The Jackson Firm came in paying a fairly good wage. When they found some of the women could make ten dollars a week, a new forelady came bringing a cut in wages. At present another change of management and another cut in wages, but I hear nothing from you, no protest from your press or Chamber of Commerce. Some of the girls are getting as low as 1.25 per week.

Furthermore, she speculated, "licentious behavior" might be related to low wages:

> You probably heard the Rev. Mr. Stevens, of tabernacle fame, make the remark from his pulpit, that Traverse City was the most licentious of any town he had ever been in, that licentiousness lurked on every street corner. …What is the cause? Is it the low wages paid your women and girls?

The *Traverse City Press* served as a place for women workers to vent their anger at low wages and lack of respect. Such a forum could not continue. Soon the *Press* began to complain of boycotts directed towards its advertisers. Abruptly, the radical tone of letters vanished. The paper itself underwent a name change to the *Grand Traverse Press*. Even in that form it did not publish long, disappearing some time around 1920.

Letters such as the one printed above paint a different picture of Traverse City from that displayed to summer visitors. It simply was not a sunny town of cherry orchards, resorts, gorgeous beaches, and picturesque winters. It had a dark side, too, with its factories that promised repetitive work for poor wages, a female workforce that was paid less than that of men for the same work, and the prospect of dismal room-and-board arrangements. A state report issued in 1917 lists Traverse City dead last in Michigan for average wages paid to workers. The 1914 Polk directory, a reference book giving names and occupations of residents, tells us that forty percent of people over fourteen years of age were listed as boarders, i.e. they did not live independently in their own residences. Even taking into account the early broad definition of "boarder" (boarders could be students or grown children), this figure illustrates the sorry living conditions of many workers. Clearly, homeowners and the people they took in had little money to spend on extras. Life was not easy here.

Edward Lautner, socialist mayor of Traverse City, 1917 (Traverse Area Historical Society)

Perhaps it is natural for a community to want to put its best foot forward, especially when visitors come calling so often. The *Traverse City Record-Eagle* would not wish to air the grievances of working men and women. Though disclaiming bias, it had a long history of working with the major players of the town—the Hannahs, the Millikens, the Hamiltons, and the Hulls. It would not want to go against the interests of businesses that advertised so regularly within its pages. Instead, the early *Traverse City Press* and, later, *Honest Opinion* would have to bear the burden of providing an open forum for all the citizens of the community. Today we recall their valiant efforts with respect, understanding the importance of listening to the voices of all residents—those of workers, businessmen, veterans, pacifists, the uneducated and the educated. It is only through such discourse that we advance as a community and as a nation.

Traverse City Fourth of July parade, 1911 (Traverse Area Historical Society)

CHAPTER 3

Celebrating the Fourth in Northwestern Michigan
A Historic Remembrance

It was to be a Grand Festival of Fun, the greatest celebration ever known in Northern Michigan. And, in spite of the rain that poured down in the morning of July 4, 1899, it was. The nation was bursting with patriotism and pride, the battle for Cuba having been won, the flag of the United States flying over that country and over Hawaii and the Philippines. The nation was ready to celebrate the dawning of the new century to come, America's century.

Traverse City was the center of the party. There would be swimming and sailing races on the Bay, foot races on Union Street for the fleet, stilt races for the acrobatic, and wheelbarrow and sack races for those unafraid of public embarrassment. Good money and public acclaim would be paid the victors in all sports. For those preferring the excitement and wagering of the track, horse racing was offered at the Driving Park, located at the present Civic Center.

There was more. The Traverse City Hustlers would go up against the Grand Rapids Democrats in a baseball game that would demonstrate the virtue of local ball players on the field south of Twelfth Street. Best of all, next to that venue, Miss Mabel Belmont would ascend five thousand feet under her smoke balloon [smoke balloon: a balloon inflated by a smoky fire set on the ground] while mounted on a bicycle, leap from on high with her parachute, and descend slowly, detaching herself from her wheel at the last moment, and land safely within a prescribed circle. It was to be one of the most daring feats ever performed here or elsewhere.

The rain did put a damper on some events, but a clearing sky later in the day saved the grand parade, the calithumpian [calithump: to make boisterous entertainment with bells, whistles, tin pots and the like] antics of those who enjoy raucous fun, the baseball game, Miss Belmont's ascension, and a spectacular fireworks display, the likes of which had never been seen in these parts. Nothing so trivial as a spot of rain could quell the patriotic spirit of the revelers.

In short, the day was a grand success. The parade's seven bands played tirelessly and with skill, the floats filed by much as they do today at the Cherry Festival (though pulled by horses), marching rows of soldiers recently returned from Cuba received the cheers of the crowd, and hundreds of children waved flags given to them for the occasion. The Hustlers triumphed 1-0 at the Twelfth Street field, with a huge crowd at hand to watch both the game and Miss Belmont's performance. While her act did not go wholly to plan, it provided thrills to the crowd.

Because weather conditions did not allow the balloon to reach its advertised five thousand foot altitude, she was forced to do her act from a height estimated at 1200 feet. Ascent went as expected, but upon leaping away from the balloon and deploying her parachute, she was unable to free herself from her wheel. As a result, in the words of Thomas T. Bates, the editor of the *Morning Record*, "...when she came down, bicycle, parachute, and the girl came down in a heap." Fortunately, she sustained but a slight bruise.

This was not the only Fourth of July spectacular that was staged in Northwestern Lower Michigan. In 1906 Elk Rapids held a celebration that included not only running and sailing events but also a Wild West Show. Perhaps drawing on elements of Buffalo Bill's Wild West Circus (which came to Traverse City in 1898), the plot of the show described events far removed from this area: A covered wagon is attacked by "Indians" and the whites are defeated in the subsequent battle. Victims are scalped and the pioneer is tied to a stake to be burned. Unsurprisingly, a band of cowboys appears at the last moment and drives the Indians away amid volleys of shots fired by both sides. The newspaper reporter covering the event notes that "no one felt very badly for some of the dead, even though they had been scalped, because several of them being unable to get a good view of the show from where they were lying would get up and look on." It was a story of another place and time and did not describe the history of contacts between the Odawa people and white settlers locally. However it did reinforce myths about Indians and whites that were propagated by Buffalo Bill's Wild West Show and popular novels, myths that persist today.

The close of the First World War was cause for further celebration. July 4, 1918, the first Farmer's Fourth of July Picnic and Celebration was held at the present Civic Center in Traverse City. It featured the usual horseracing, baseball, and foot race events as well as something novel and exciting: a demonstration of a recent invention, the tractor. Though noisy, a fleet of them accomplished agricultural feats more efficiently than horses, tilling, raking, and planting in a confusion of exhaust and backfire. In awe of the machines and the festival itself, the *Record-Eagle*'s bold headline for July 5th proclaimed its success:

Twelve Thousand Gather Here for General Observance of a Patriotically Sane Fourth

The use of the phrase "patriotically sane" requires explanation. From early in the nineteenth century the Fourth was a time to shoot guns and display fireworks, both privately and publicly. Young people would purchase quantities of firecrackers, bombs, and rockets for their own delight, setting them off in ways hazardous to themselves and others. Traverse City's City Bookstore advertised a giant stock of fireworks ranging from penny firecrackers to one dollar explosives (which must have contained a window-rattling charge of powder!). One visitor to the United States in the 1800's observed, "A pall of gunpowder hung over cities and villages throughout the day as men and boys expressed their noisy pleasure in independence." No doubt in its enthusiasm for detonations Traverse City was no different from other towns across the country.

By 1908 opposition to the noise, injuries, and fires caused by fireworks resulted in a national campaign, the Safe and Sane Fourth. By publishing the number of fireworks fatalities and injuries nationwide, it caught people's attention as it promoted alternative means of celebrating the holiday: parades, music, pageants, and, indeed, events like the Farmer's Fourth of July Picnic and Celebration. Four years earlier, the editor of the *Record-Eagle,* Thomas T. Bates, praised the movement towards a quieter Fourth: "The safe and sane celebration has come to stay, and while some may regret the passing of the old system of observing the day, the change is for the common good." While the Fourth still had its share of explosions and rockets, the din had subsided considerably. A "safe and sane" holiday was in sight. Indeed, in 1929 the Michigan legislature banned the detonation of fireworks except by trained technicians contracted by cities and townships.

Aside from the balloon ascensions and parades, the Wild West Shows and competitions, there was always another side to the holiday. July 4th marked the beginning of summer. Picnics, family outings, and excursions to scenic places were popular activities from the very beginning of our nation. On Independence Day 1906 twelve hundred people visited Bassett's Island, crossing over to Marion Island with their picnic lunches for a day of relaxation. Boats ran every hour all day long, carrying loads of passengers from Traverse City and back, the last heading back to the city at 1:30, full of revelers exhausted from dancing and partying. Having endured the endless frosty days of winter, this Northern Michigan town welcomed the warm, sunny days to come. It was not just patriotism that people celebrated. It was summer itself.

Besides rejoicing in the season, what exactly were people celebrating on the 4th? The nation's Centennial, 1876, was celebrated in Charlevoix by orations and grove exercises, performances in which patriotic readings and recitations played an important part. Following that, the crowd would enjoy tub-racing, auger-racing, wheelbarrow racing, horseracing, greased pig, and a balloon ascension. Patriotic readings and speeches centered about the events surrounding July 4, 1776, were common throughout the nineteenth century. By the first decade of the twentieth century, they had largely disappeared, losing out in the popularity contest to athletic competitions, balloon ascensions, and, perhaps, the greased pig. Still, the War of Independence was remembered as late as 1918, if not in orations, then in print. Julius Steinberg, a well-known entrepreneur of Traverse City, placed a large advertisement in the Record-Eagle that year asking the community to remember Washington, Ethan Allen and the Green Mountain Boys, Valley Forge, Patrick Henry, Lafayette, and all the others that had contributed to our nation's birth.

With the Spanish-American War the tone of the holiday shifted, now emphasizing the power and prestige of the United States as well as rejoicing in its newly acquired empire. America was the original modern democracy and it would spread its values throughout the world. Truly, God had blessed America and now America would uplift and convert the world to its way of life. World War I only increased its resolve to "make the world safe for democracy."

How odd that end of World War II did not bring about the same patriotic celebrations that World War I did. The Fourths of 1945 and 1946 were unremarkable in Traverse City, no competitions, no parades, no fireworks, though several smaller communities did sponsor patriotic activities, sometimes connected with a local festival. Nearby Suttons Bay, for example, offered a full day's entertainment culminating in fireworks in the evening in conjunction with its annual Homecoming festivities. That same year, Manistee put on a floral parade and Mummer's parade as it celebrated the Fourth and the Manistee National Forest Festival.

The driving force behind these events was not patriotic, but commercial. The economy of Northern Michigan was dependent on the yearly influx of tourists and the Fourth was the beginning of it all. That is not to say commercialism was absent from early celebrations of the Fourth. In 1899 visitors came to Traverse City from all over Northern Michigan to join in the fun. Hotels were filled and local businesses profited from the increased human traffic. Accounts of the 1904 celebration in Elk Rapids spoke of the large numbers of Traverse City people in attendance, some no doubt ready to

Early postcard view of Bassett Island showing the dock, pavilion, and a visiting steamer. Orson W. Peck, 1906 (Traverse Area Historical Society)

spend a dollar on a souvenir or a meal. Aside from honoring the nation's birthday, the extravagant festivals of the past lured visitors to villages and towns situated at the end of a long peninsula, places that saw few travelers during the long winter months. Then as now, it was natural that July 4th would signal the beginning of tourist season as well as stand as a day of national pride.

Now, since in recent years the Cherry Festival has become linked with the Fourth, Traverse City celebrations resemble those of the past. Mile runs, long distance runs, cherry pie eating contests, the milk jug regatta and other foolery, parades with miles of floats, and fireworks both on the Fourth and at the end of the Cherry Festival remind us of the extravaganzas of 1899 and 1918. On alternate years the Blue Angels precision flying team entertains crowds numbered in the hundreds of thousands. At times it is hard to separate the patriotic elements: veterans marching in formation, patriotic music, flags always in view, and the Blue Angels overhead, from the commercial: T-shirt vendors, floats promoting the Blueberry Festival and the like, the Cherry Queen and her entourage, the midway, and the sellers of brats, deep-fried turkey legs, elephant ears, and cotton candy. That is the way it has always been for the Fourth of July in this part of Michigan: a mixture of patriotism and summer fun.

CHAPTER 4

From Doctor's Visits to the Modern Hospital
How Medical Care has Changed in the Traverse Area

1908, Traverse City, Michigan: A woman with a sick child. A young man with a sprained ankle. An old man suffering from tuberculosis. A girl with a persistent sore throat. How did they receive medical care? Where did they meet their doctors? How did they get their medicines? What did they believe about disease? Exactly how was medicine practiced at this time when the settlement of Traverse City, barely fifty years old, was growing rapidly in population and importance?

You can get a picture of early medical practice in Traverse City by examining *Evening Record* and other newspaper advertising. At the same time, by looking at modern medical practice, you can understand the changes that have occurred over the past hundred years in medicine. Those changes go beyond advances in high-tech scanning technology, heart monitors, new kinds of anesthesia, DNA testing, and "miracle drugs." They touch upon the way society regards the medical profession and the beliefs people hold about the causes, prevention and treatment of disease.

Even in its isolated location, Traverse City is a model of the larger changes that were affecting medicine worldwide. To discover local traces of these dramatic changes in medicine—the germ theory of disease, patient treatment moving from home to clinic, improved training of doctors, science-based medicine dominating all other alternative forms of care—let us look at the way early medicine was practiced in Northern Michigan one hundred years ago.

Patent Medicines a Hundred Years Ago

Medicine-related advertising in the *Evening Record* of 1908 was plentiful. While drug companies and patent medicine firms have largely abandoned newspapers as an advertising medium in recent years, before the days of radio and television, ads for cough medicine, nerve tonics, kidney and liver nostrums, blood thinners and purifiers, relief for menstrual difficulties, and calmatives for stomach and bowel distress filled newspaper pages. Regularly, the paper featured six, eight, ten or more such advertisements, some taking up two columns of space and extending ten inches or more down the page. In general they promised no cures for major diseases of the time—pneumonia, heart disease, influenza, tuberculosis—though they did offer symptomatic relief for those afflicted with the discomforts of human existence—the coughs, indigestion, rheumatism, the ever present fatigue and listlessness that shadows the lives of many over the course of their lives. Some were, no doubt, successful. Cherry cough syrup did quiet coughing, at least in the short term. Senna laxatives were effective, if sometimes harsh. And Kodol's dyspepsia pills might have soothed an unhappy stomach.

On the other hand, many advertised medicines obtained their reputation through the placebo effect. Believing "Mother's Friend" to be effective in "shortening the duration of labor" or in "assisting in the safe and quick delivery," some lucky mothers saw apparent benefit to the medicine even if it had no physical effect. Nerve tonics, blood purifiers, and medicines designed to cure alcoholism were like this, the endless newspaper testimonials of satisfied customers readily convincing the gullible. Often advertisements simulated news stories, the reader tricked into reading a story with an ordinary headline followed by an article printed in the font regularly used by the newspaper. Seeing through such attempts to provide a veneer of respectability on these curatives, physicians of the time (as well as many citizens) regarded the most outrageous claims of the advertisements as quackery. Supposedly effective against the "alcohol habit," Orrine was castigated by Indiana State Food and Drug Commissioner H.E. Barnard as a worthless concoction of 82% sugar solution, a salt of ammonium, and a trace of gold (!) chloride, a mixture that costs the maker only a few pennies. Such fakery was repeated in hundreds of medicines across the country. Though truth-in-labeling laws were passed in 1906, it would take twenty-five more years before deceptive advertisements were banished from newspapers.

The purveyors of over-the-counter nostrums often took the position that their medications did not cure anything, but simply helped a person remain healthy. Medicines should be taken occasionally to maintain good health, not to cure illness. In the late nineteenth and early twentieth century world of Traverse City, the pathway to good health was clear, even if the treatment of disease was not. Healthy living involved fresh air, sunshine, and clean homes, yards, and streets. While describing germs as a cause

An advertisement for Lydia E. Pinkham's Vegetable Compound. Note the resemblance of the ad to an ordinary news story.

of contagion, general science books still advocated sanitation as a means of preventing disease. Although Pasteur's germ theory of disease had gained general acceptance, the prior idea that disease grows out of filth was deeply rooted in people's minds. In fact, while clean water does prevent the spread of typhoid and other water-borne diseases, removal of dirt by itself does little to prevent disease. Like cleanliness, regular doses of patent medicines were seen by some as another factor necessary to good health and they were cheaper. Barnard writes in 1917:

> ...they [false advertising laws] cannot prevent the credulous who still think of medicine as a form of "Black Art" from falling into the error that a bottle of medicine is as good as a doctor's visit and costs less."

Where Medicine Was Practiced: Homes, Doctor's Offices, and Hospitals

Barnard's phrase "doctor's visit" points to the prevailing way medicine was practiced in the early years of the twentieth century. Home visits by the doctor were common and many doctors would give their own residence address in case the office was closed and an emergency arose. For the most part medicine was not carried on in the antiseptically clean rooms of a hospital or clinic, but in drawing rooms and bedrooms of patients and receiving rooms of doctors. Doctors, families, and patients interacted with each other informally, sharing stories and histories as friends without the status differences that obtrude in the doctor-patient relationship nowadays. There were few secrets between doctor, family and friends; medical privacy was unknown. Late in her life, Traverse City's pioneer doctor Augusta Rosenthal-Thompson described this relaxed give-and-take doctor-patient relationship:

> ...I soon found that when I had a child to care for, I also had the rest of the family as patients—and friends.

While advanced technology and notions about efficiency have made home practice rare in modern times, nostalgia for old ways persists. The image of the doctor as friend and equal does not die easily.

Though doctors in the Traverse area primarily carried on their practice in drawing rooms and their own offices, hospitals were to be found in the area in 1908. The biggest of these was the Grand Traverse Hospital, located on the Bay near the junction of M-22 and M-72. It could accommodate as many as nineteen patients, though an average of ten beds were filled at a time. Two hundred three patients were admitted in one year, a figure quoted in the newspaper to impress readers by its immensity. Besides patient care facilities, an immaculate operating room was maintained, done in white with acetylene lights as well as a droplight that could be moved to any location around the operating table. Within a year one hundred ten operations were performed, sixty-one of them termed major and forty-nine minor. Only four obstetrical cases were recorded.

The figures quoted here raise questions about hospital care at the turn of the century. The *Evening Record* declares "Few towns of the size of Traverse City can boast so good a place for caring for the sick as the Grand Traverse Hospital," indicating this facility was of better quality than many in the area. Still, nineteen beds is a small hospital by any standard today. Two hundred admissions a year seems absurdly low for a town of nearly twelve thousand people as does sixty-nine serious operations in a twelve month period. Clearly hospitals a hundred years ago were different institutions from their descendents of the twenty-first century.

How were they different? First, it should be noted that, for the most part, babies were not delivered in hospitals. Four obstetrical cases in a year imply that only a few deliveries, perhaps those with anticipated complications, were done in a hospital setting. Second, a figure given in the newspaper for 'moribunds' (those who died within forty-eight hours of admittance) was ten. Thus, with five percent of admissions for the dying, the hospital was not where most people came to die. The poor were admitted to the hospital at County expense, though exact numbers of these admissions are not given. Whatever the number, the charitable function of the institution is underlined by the presence of the indigent sick.

In summary, hospitals a hundred years ago were not for births or deaths or convalescence from illness (except for the poor). Operations were performed there and people needed some recovery time in the hospital. In the years before advances in medi-

Grand Traverse Hospital, located just north of the intersection of the Grandview Parkway and M72. (Traverse Area Historical Society)

cal technology, treatment and healing could take place at home as well as in the hospital. In fact, hospitals played a significant role in spreading contagious diseases. Shortly before its destruction by fire in 1913, the Grand Traverse Hospital had plans to build a separate cottage to house those with diseases easily transmitted to other patients. In the late nineteenth century, it was not unusual for hospitals to be burned to the ground in order to construct a new building upon the sterile ashes. For patients, hospitals could be (and still are!) dangerous places.

Doctors: Of Their Gender, Specialties, and Medical Training

The *Evening Record* of 1908 displays advertisements for ten doctors. Surprisingly, in an age of male privilege, two of them—Sara T. Chase and Augusta Rosenthal-Thompson—were women. Of the ten, four doctors declared they possessed an M.D., though others may have held the degree without stating so. Four of the advertisements directed the reader's attention to the doctor's ability to fit eyeglasses, perhaps indicating that that specialty was especially lucrative. Two were surgeon-physicians and one (Rosenthal-Thompson) specialized in diseases of women and children, while another advertised his specialization in diseases of the genito-urinary and skin systems as well as diseases of the blood. Other doctors were certainly practicing in Traverse City at this time—the Polk Directory lists seventeen of them including two osteopaths—but they did not seek out new patients in the *Evening Record*. One was associated with the only hospital listed for Traverse City at this time, the Grand Traverse Hospital. In addition, several physician assistants as well as Dr. James Decker Munson, served at the Northern Michigan Asylum. They did not see patients from the area.

In 1908 the medical profession was just emerging from a shadowy past. In the middle of the nineteenth century enormous numbers of doctors were trained in medical schools that survived and even prospered by student tuition. Training was abominable with prospective physicians entering medical school sometimes without even a high school diploma, sitting through as little as eight months of academic classes and graduating without sufficient experience in clinical and hospital practice. Problems were most acute in the southern states, though low standards could be found everywhere. Abraham Flexner in his critical report to the Rockefeller Foundation, *Medical Education in the United States and Canada,* reported that Michigan, though it supported one of the best medical schools in the country, the University of Michigan, still allowed unqualified doctors to practice medicine. Surprisingly, the University of Michigan Medical School provided support for the Michigan School of Homeopathy, an institution of doubtful scientific standing, until 1922. In short, doctors in the late nineteenth and early twentieth centuries were less educated than professionals of other occupations and did not receive the respect accorded them now. Though Michigan had more stringent licensing requirements than many other states, it still had a number of ill-trained doctors in practice educated in other states as well as in Michigan. In 1908 Traverse City, like most American cities, was in the process of redefining the status of medical doctors. It would be the middle of the century before they obtained the respect given to them now.

Medicine Then and Now: Explaining the Differences

Today medicine is a vastly different enterprise than it was at the beginning of the last century. Above all, it is bigger. Even taking population growth and regionalization of services into account, society devotes more of its resources towards health care. Munson Medical Center reports that more than four hundred physicians from fifty-seven specialties are affiliated with the hospital, a shocking contrast to the ten physicians from four specialties advertising in the *Evening Record* at the turn of the last century. What accounts for this increase in physicians, facilities, and expenditures on health matters? Does it simply relate to advanced medical technology and greater wealth enjoyed by more people?

Certainly advanced technology plays a role in expanding the medical industry. Certain physician specializations have evolved since 1908 primarily due to technology: radiology and anesthesiology, to name two. And people with more money to spend could fuel the expansion of medicine into areas that seek to do more than simply maintain good health: plastic surgery, removal of varicose veins, and specialties that aim to enhance life styles of the wealthy. But such excursions into "superfluous medicine" cannot explain the mushroom growth of medical expenditures. Neither does the treatment of certain physical problems such as sleep disorders and obesity, conditions that were rarely dealt with through medicine. Technology, money, and the application of medicine to a new set of maladies do not explain the meteoric increase in resources devoted to medicine over the past hundred years. There is a better explanation: The increase in resources devoted to medicine in America comes from a rise in medical authority—the perception that doctors have special knowledge and skill that cannot be found elsewhere—and the empowering of that perception through exploiting the American capitalist system.

Medical authority is a concept elucidated by Paul Starr in his Pulitzer Prize winning book, *The Social Transformation of American Medicine*. In it he describes medical authority as "a surrender of private judgment." Simply put, people defer to the doctor in entertaining opinions about diagnosing and treating illnesses. That deference is based upon the undeniable successes of the medical profession over the past century. Patients find it hard to argue with a man who belongs to the profession that conquered smallpox and tuberculosis. Furthermore, by the early twentieth century, alternative forms of medicine had been marginalized: homeopathy, Christian Science, animal magnetism and other healing programs originating in other countries were practiced by a small minority of people. Mainstream medicine is, for most of the population, the only game in town. That puts it in a category by itself.

By itself, that does not explain the growth of medicine. As they gained respect within society, physicians were able to set high standards for medical schools and state licensing requirements, limit the number of medical schools, and secure medical school funding from a variety of governmental and private sources. More importantly, they could work out arrangements with hospitals and insurance companies so that they would retain their independence and receive checks for "services rendered" rather than a salary paid by an employer. The net result was that medicine became the highest paid profession, doctors receiving income above lawyers, accountants, and teachers. Unlike education, medicine adapted well to the American economic system.

In recent years the rise in power of insurance and pharmaceutical companies has cast a shadow over the previous "Golden Age" of the medical profession. Doctors are in subjugation to the demands of insurance companies and governmental programs such as Medicaid and Medicare. Now extraordinary amounts of time are spent in physicians' offices dealing with paperwork, time and effort that Dr. Chase or Dr. Rosenthal-Thompson would have found unnecessary a hundred years ago. Of course, medicine gets more done now (as it should, given the enormous resources devoted to it.) Still, by comparison to medicine as practiced in Traverse City long ago, it lacks the personal, human quality that pervaded medical practice at that time. We would not trade the medicine we have now for what we had then, but at the same time we cannot help but feel that medical practice has lost a measure of its innocence and purity since those far-off days of physician house calls made in the dead of night.

CHAPTER 5

Of Vagrants, Poor Funds and Poor Houses
Poverty a Hundred Years Ago

Over the hill to the poor-house—my chil'rn dear, good-by!
Many a night I've watched you when only God was nigh;
And God'll judge between us; but I will al'ays pray
That you shall never suffer the half I do to-day.

–Will Carleton, 1872

In 1904 the City of Traverse City gave Mrs. Amos Whitcomb forty-three dollars for food, twelve dollars for fuel, and four dollars seventy-three cents for medicine. It gave the Whitney children two dollars for food and two sixty for clothing. To Thomas Stephenson it paid costs for food, medicine, medical attendance and, eventually, funeral costs. This outlay of money to the needy was supplied by the Traverse City Poor Fund, a budget category noted in the City Annual Reports from 1898 to 1904. Though the fund disappeared from city accounts after only a few years, it represented an attempt to aid the poor of the city in an era before state and federal welfare programs existed. The short list of beneficiaries (only 53) and the tiny packages of relief they received provoke questions: In these early years of the city how did the poor survive? How widespread was poverty at the beginning of the twentieth century, both nationally and locally? Exactly who were poor? What were the reasons for their poverty? Finally, how are the poor treated now in comparison to those raw days of the past? How has the face of poverty changed over the course of a century?

In the early years of the twentieth century the poor were divided up into two classes: paupers (who did not work because of moral failings) and the "deserving poor," those that could not work because of disability, old age, accidents, etc. Within the paupers category, tramps, vagrants, and hobos comprised one large segment. As a group they received no aid from society except, perhaps, a modicum of charity from people so inclined to give. Otherwise they survived at the fringe of society, subsisting on occasional odd jobs and petty crime. By contrast, the "deserving poor" received support from various sources. Above all, the extended family of parents, grandparents, aunts and uncles would come to the rescue by offering loans, housing, food, clothing and the like. After that, churches, lodges, and trade unions would donate to help a family in financial trouble.

Institutions of the nineteenth and early twentieth century provided a safety net for some. The Northern Michigan Asylum (later, Traverse City State Hospital) would accept the poor if insanity could be demonstrated. The County would pick up the bill for these unfortunates. In addition, for the poor that suffered accidents and illness, the County would occasionally pay for treatment at the Grand Traverse Hospital, ten dollars per day. Traverse City's Poor Fund, described above, would contribute towards medical care, ambulance transportation, and medicine if required. Fuel, food, rent, and clothing would be paid out of the fund, too. It appears that most payments were made to the ill, disabled, and to widows with children.

Such help was temporary and uncertain, at least for the most part. In comparing the City Reports from 1901 to 1904, only seven names are to be found in both records. Presumably those in need of long-term financial aid would be directed to a local poorhouse. Applying for money did not necessarily mean the applicant would receive financial support. In this paternalistic age, men and women who requested funds for food, clothing, shelter and fuel could easily be turned down by the Director of the Poor for a variety of reasons. A bad reputation, a history of destitution, a poor attitude, or an unsavory appearance could and did affect a person's success in receiving funds. The Poor Fund did not guarantee assistance to all.

Mercifully, though sometimes in disregard of keeping a family together, reformatories for children—the Industrial Home for Girls at Adrian, Michigan, and the State Industrial School for Boys at Lansing—would collect neglected and poor children who committed petty crimes, some as trivial as truancy, and institutionalize them at the expense of the State in an effort to reform them through moral training and by teaching them a trade. Intended to remold young characters in an effort to prevent crime, the reformatories provided food, shelter, and medical care for helpless youth.

Counties ran their own poorhouses. Opened in 1911, the Boardman Valley Hospital (also known as Grand Traverse Sanitarium, the County Poor House, and Grand Traverse County Hospital) served as both a poorhouse and a hospital. While it had rooms outfitted for childbirth and surgery, it also had a farm that was operated by residents who were committed there. Who were they? We can identify twenty-three persons by using the 1920 census, twenty-one men and only two women. Looking at the records of the Allegan Poorhouse, we can get a sense of who lived at that facility in 1900 and 1910. There were the elderly, one as old as ninety-seven years old. There were the blind; four lived at Allegan in 1910. Most likely there were the so-called feebleminded as well as those with physical disabilities, this conclusion drawn from records at other facilities. There were widows without children as well as widows with surviving children who were unable to support their mother. In short, assuming conditions were similar here, the indigent housed at the Boardman Valley Hospital were there for a variety of reasons.

Poverty was common in Grand Traverse County and in the United States in the early years of the twentieth century. Robert Hunter wrote in his 1905 book *Poverty* that twelve percent of the American population was in poverty. His criterion of 460 dollars

The Boardman Valley Hospital was located on Cass Road upon property now occupied by the school bus garage. This picture was taken after its abandonment in 1959. (*Preview*)

per year for a family of five is now widely recognized as too low. James T. Patterson, a modern writer on poverty, suggests a figure of seven hundred dollars per year would offer a more appropriate comparison to poverty levels experienced in the nineteen seventies. Using Patterson's higher figure, about forty percent of the American population was below the poverty level in 1900.

How poor was Grand Traverse County at this time? There is no reason to think the poverty rate was different from the rest of the country as a whole. Forty-two percent of the persons listed in the 1904 Polk Directory (a volume which gives information about city residents) were "boarders." They lived as adult members of a household (some having finished school at age 14) and did not own property. Many were retail clerks, laborers, students, and teachers. For the most part, their scant possessions could be contained in a packing trunk. Though most could escape starvation and the cold, there were few amenities in their lives.

Most local residents in poverty were employed, at least for portions of the year, but wages were low. The largest employer in Traverse City, the Oval Wood Dish Company, paid male workers one dollar and forty-four cents per day before a one day strike in 1912. The company ran a nine hour day at this time, six days a week. Allowing for a few holidays within the year, workers would take home about four hundred fifty dollars a year, well below the poverty level at this time. And women received less pay than men. Considering that the Oval Wood Dish Company hired forty percent of non-farm laborers by some estimates, it is clear that workers here were living at the brink of economic disaster.

Who were the poor? The despised pauper class, those unwilling to do work, comprised about twelve percent, by some estimates. The rest were workers who earned low wages, the unemployed, the disabled, the elderly, and, above all, dependents: women and children. Besides workers earning low wages, farmers were even worse off. Nationally, Hunter notes that fifty-two percent of them did not even own their farms. Unemployment made it impossible for workers to get out of their economic abyss. Twenty-two percent of workers in New York City were unemployed for a period of time in a single year. Above all, the poor were dependent upon others for survival. Edward Devine, another early writer on poverty, declared that fully two-thirds of the poor were women and children. It was a perception that was not understood by the public at the time. Though they accepted that bad things can happen to good people, they still tended to see the poor in terms of the hobo, the vagrant, the lazy, the drunkard, and the profligate.

In the nineteenth century people attributed most social ills—including poverty—to individual moral failing. Adult criminals come from a criminal class in which lawlessness is the norm. The insane derive their sorry condition from misbehavior of parents who passed along their failings through genetic inheritance. The sick—at least in part—suffered because they did not practice good hygiene. And the poor—at least a fair number of them—had mainly themselves to blame for their poverty for lack of prudence, industry, and financial judgment. Society as a whole did not accept responsibility for these problems. Lack of education, unemployment, the stress of overwork, low wages, and unhealthful living conditions were largely ignored as writers and politicians pointed their fingers at individual weaknesses and bad decisions on a wide scale. As a consequence of this "blame the individual" attitude, outdoor relief (now called welfare) was curtailed at the end of the nineteenth century in many large cities. The prevailing belief was that paying money to the poor only enabled their habits of dependency. Repudiated in the nineteen thirties, this view staged a comeback during the nineteen eighties and nineties as the stereotype of the "Welfare Cadillac," (mainly black women who received welfare and managed to bilk the system of enough money to buy a Cadillac), gained traction among the voting public. In attributing poverty to individual moral failing, it was a rerun of social prejudices that existed at the end of the nineteenth century.

In the beginning poverty was considered a local problem. Communities would deal with it as they could with tax collections, charity, and fundraising activities designed to help those in need. Counties established poor houses in the nineteenth century and contributed money to support inmates in asylums, jails, and reformatories. If an indigent person required medical care in a hospital, the County would pay for it—at least for a few days. The locus of care began with individual responsibility, extended to the family, and later came to include the County and State. In the nineteen thirties the federal government entered the picture with Social Security, unemployment insurance, and other programs that offered relief to the poor. However, welfare reform measures passed in the nineteen nineties returned responsibility to the states as the federal government provided block grants to states to implement programs that benefit the poor.

Compared to a hundred years ago, there is more governmental help available to the poor. Social Security retirement, Social Security disability, Medicare, Medicaid, SCHIP for children's medical care, unemployment insurance, Earned Income Tax Credits, Temporary Assistance For Needy Families, Food Stamps and other federal and state programs provide a modest safety net for those in financial trouble. In recent years there has been a shrinkage in governmental programs and a growth in nonprofit programs such as Goodwill and the Salvation Army. Now as formerly there is a tension between the view that poverty is an outcome of a failure in personal morality or a failure of society to provide decent jobs, health care for all, a good education for poor children, and programs to rehabilitate persons that occupy the lowest places in the community. The pendulum has swung from a glimpse of the welfare state in the sixties to a reliance on individualism and private charity in the eighties and nineties. As we go through bad times and good, Americans will try to find a balance between individual responsibility and societal obligation with regard to helping the poor. That is the way it has always been in the Traverse area and nation-wide, a hundred years ago to the present.

A row of maple trees possibly planted in honor of WWI veterans located just south of the Garfield Township Hall. (Author photo)

CHAPTER 6

The Veterans Memorial Highway

Rediscovering Living Monuments to
Spanish-American and World War I Soldiers

> *A song for the heroes gone on ahead*
> *To join the hosts of the marching dead—*
> *A song for the souls that could lightly fling*
> *Sweet life away as a little thing*
> *For the sake of the mighty need of earth,*
> *The need of the ages coming to birth.*
> *Glory that God gathers the heroes home*
> *Out of the red fields, out of the foam,*
> *Gathers them out of the Everywhere*
> *Into the Camp that is Over There.*
> –Edwin Markham

From a plaque erected at the Grand Traverse Courthouse
honoring veterans of the Spanish-American War dated May 30, 1924.

The April 25, 1923 *Record-Eagle* proclaimed in a bold headline "Memorial Tree Will Be Placed For Each Hero," later explaining that veterans who lost their lives during the Spanish-American or the World War would have maple trees planted in honor of their sacrifice. The highway entering town from the south, then called Highway 11 and now Veterans Drive, would be designated a Memorial Highway. Each tree would be dedicated to a veteran who had died during his service to the country during the two wars. In later newspaper stories it was announced that three stone memorials with bronze plaques would be placed in the Traverse area, one at the top of Rennie Hill and the other two at the Courthouse. They would tell the purpose of the memorial and would list the names of the soldiers who had died.

The article provokes questions. Do any of the trees still remain? What of planting trees to remember the war dead—was that something widely practiced at this time? And the plaques themselves—where are they now, more than eighty-five years after they were laid? By reading newspaper accounts, listening to the recollections of knowledgeable people, and simply making good observations, a history sleuth can get answers to such questions.

A quick inspection reveals that few maples of the proper size and age line Veterans Drive near the Garfield Township Hall. However, at the edge of the Memorial Gardens Cemetery property stands a row of five trees, all maples and very large. They are in decline, troubled with peeling bark and dead branches, but they could be remnants of the original forty-three trees. It is true that they do not exactly parallel the asphalt roadbed nearby, but the direction of the road could have been altered since 1924, thus accounting for the misalignment. Mysteriously, one of them has metal hardware embedded in it—perhaps a sign of some sort used to hang there. Was it a sign that told of the Memorial Highway?

Traffic from the south entering the city went down Rennie Hill to Fourteenth Street and then proceeded to Front Street by Union or Cass. This highway was the west branch of the Dixie Highway, an early interstate route which began at Sault St. Marie and ended more than two thousand miles away in Florida. At the time, it was the pride of the State and of Northern Michigan. One of Traverse City's most important citizens, Frank Hamilton, had championed its construction from its beginning in 1915.

The Dixie Highway was dedicated as a Memorial Highway with sections of it planted with trees commemorating war veterans. It is not to be confused with "Blue Star Memorial Highways," a nationwide program that sought to honor World War II vets. M-31 entering the City from the south was designated a part of that network. Signs, roadside parks, and plantings marked Blue Star Highways in the same manner as the various Memorial Highways that commemorated the sacrifice of vets from the First World War.

Along the Dixie Highway, maintenance of tree plantings was required of the counties through which the highway passed. Grand Traverse County would care for the Memorial trees south of town while City groups, especially women's clubs, would erect bronze plaques to honor the fallen soldiers both near the tree-lined avenue and at a prominent civic location.

President Warren G. Harding advocated planting trees to remember the war dead. He once said, "A general adoption of the [tree planting] plan would, in the coming years, be noted as one of the useful and beautiful ideas which our soldiers brought back from France. The splendid avenues of France have been among the great delights of the travelers there, and a similar development would equally add to the beauty and attraction of our country." The avenues of France were apparently the inspiration for the trees that were planted locally.

There were three plaques cast to recognize veterans at this time, two mounted upon shafts standing at either side of the sidewalk leading to the Courthouse off Washington Street and the other upon a granite boulder at the top of Rennie Hill. Originally situated at the Garfield Township Hall, that plaque now can be found at the V.F.W. Hall, several blocks south. It reads:

> This tablet was erected by the people of the Grand Traverse region to commemorate the first planting and dedication of trees on Memorial Avenue May 4, 1923, to the honor of all her boys and girls who served in the World War. Promoted by the County Federation of women's clubs and organizations.

A memorial plaque dedicated to the veterans of WWI, presently located at the VFW Hall on Veterans Drive. (Author photo)

The other two plaques at the Courthouse listed eight soldiers lost in the Spanish-American War and forty-five who perished in the World War. One of the forty-five was James F. Munson, the only son of James Decker Munson, the founder of Munson Hospital and first superintendent of the Northern Michigan Asylum. Along with many others, he died as a result of the flu pandemic rather than combat wounds. That disease killed many more young people than bullets, bombs and mustard gas.

And so the remaining maple trees of Veterans Drive age and wither. At the same time, our memories of those early wars fade away as friends and relatives of veterans die. A bronze plaque on a granite boulder, plaques upon stone shafts at the Courthouse, trees that barely withstand the salt of winter highway upkeep—there is pathos in these reminders of our past. Let us resolve to keep alive the memories of these soldiers of distant wars. Their sacrifice, so honored within their lifetimes, should not be forgotten.

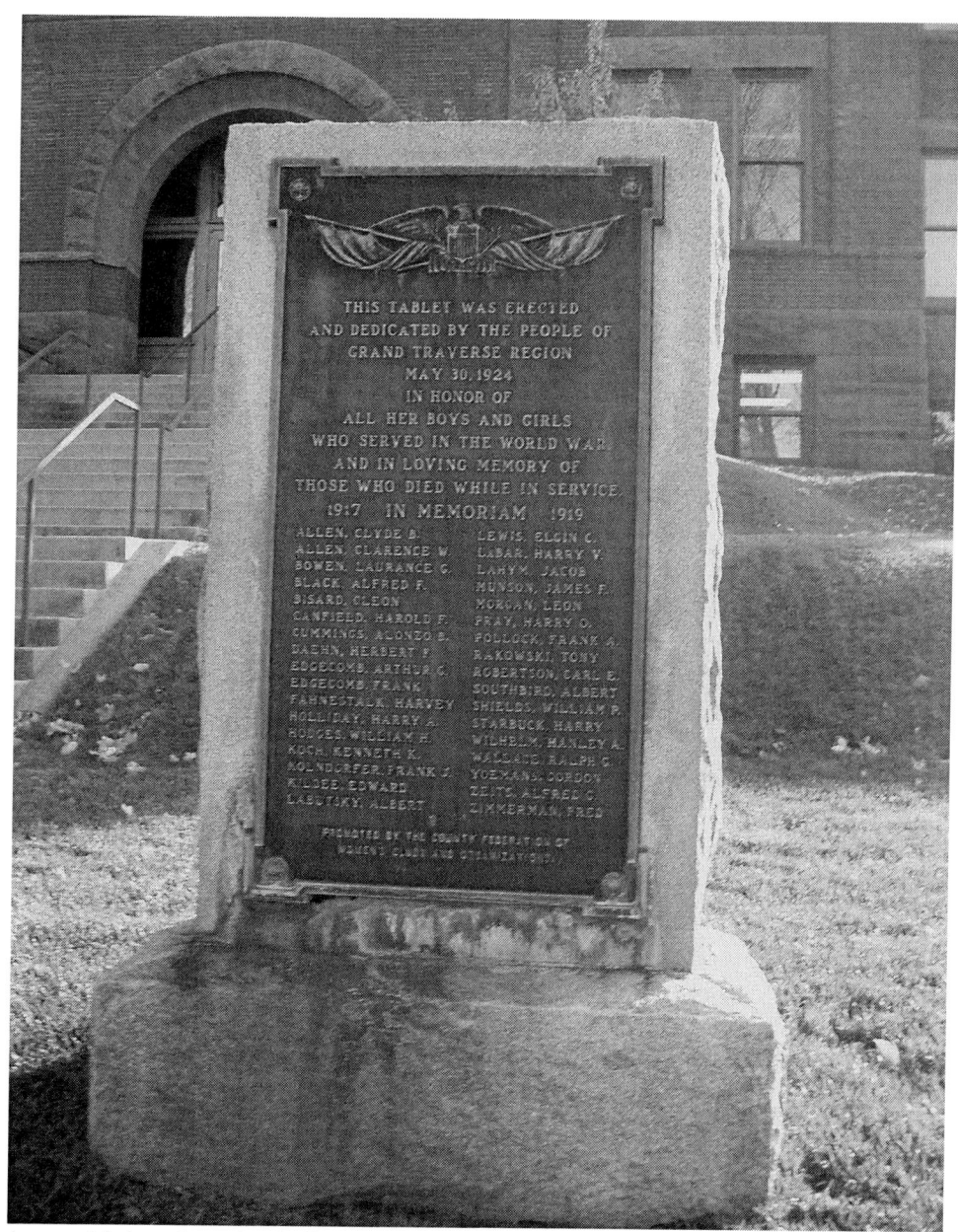

A memorial plaque located at the Traverse City Courhouse. (Author photo)

The inscription on the back of this photograph reads "Traverse City County Jail, 1892." (Traverse Area Historical Society)

CHAPTER 7

Crime and Justice a Century Ago
Examining the Jail Record of Grand Traverse County

Bound in leather, its cover filled with faded ornamentations in gold, the book rests on a table in the hushed space of the Michigan Archives. Loose strings dangle from the binding as it is opened yet again, the continual imposition of human fingers having burst the spine after more than a hundred years of use. A gorgeous book paper displays itself on the inside of the cover, and then the pages follow—288 of them—without the yellowing or foxing of old age, the unbleached white little changed since 1870. Upon their ruled faces, penned entries in a variety of hands fill 177 pages of the book. These pages, smudged with the oils of countless hands, speak to us now across the wide gulf of time that separates the lives of the writers from our own, telling us things about the society that gave rise to our own, and answering some of the questions that we have the courage to ask.

This is the *Jail Record of Grand Traverse County*, a book that records the names of those arrested in the County, dates of arrest beginning in 1870 and ending in 1906, crimes committed, occupations, race, sex, ages, birthplaces and other personal information, as well as the subsequent disposition of the cases in court. It is one of a few such books that remain in the Archives, most having been disposed of by county law enforcement agencies after new formats for recording information had been instituted. How fortunate we are to have the book available to us! It contains a treasure of information for those who would explore its pages.

The questions we ask about events are not always the same questions participants in the past would ask. For example, the *Jail Record* records information about the prisoners' national origins, literacy, drinking habits, and means of making a living. The descriptive words are not those we would use today: "mulatto" describes race, while "Asian" is left out; "temperate, (does not drink)" "intemperate," (drinks in moderation) and "drunkard" (alcoholic) inform us of the person's attitude towards alcohol; "laborer" denotes someone without formal training who performs physical work; "tramp" or "vagrant" is used for the unemployed and homeless. A hundred years ago there was little concern about privacy, racial stereotyping, or ethnic prejudice. On the other hand, foreign origins, adultery, and bastardy (making a woman pregnant and not providing support to the child), were subjects law enforcement paid careful attention to. In examining these old records, it is important to understand the world as the accused criminals, the police, and contemporary society experienced it. Our present-day emphasis on avoiding moral judgment was unknown at the time the *Jail Record* was filled out. At that time, moral judgment was very much what the law was about.

✣

What about those arrested at the turn of the twentieth century—who were they? What were they arrested for? These questions demand immediate answers, but we must inquire more deeply: What are we to make of the criminal justice system as it existed long ago? How is it different from our present system? In short, after making sense out of it, we need to reflect upon significance of this old record book. After all, history without reflection is only sterile description.

Those arrested at the beginning of the twentieth century were predominantly poor white men. They were laborers and farmers with a sprinkling of workers in the trades as well as the unemployed. Professionals—doctors, veterinarians, engineers, teachers, lawyers—are hardly represented at all and there are no arrest records of merchants. One is struck by the apparent virtue of the upper middle class. Could they have been so spotless in conduct as the record implies? Did they do their crimes out of sight of the law? Or, were they sent home if drunk and disorderly or allowed to pay money to keep out of jail? The answer probably draws upon each of the possibilities. Crime rates are lower among the more affluent, criminal behavior among them is kept off the street, and they have the financial and persuasive means to avoid arrest. In his book, *Crime and Punishment In American History*, Lawrence M. Friedman writes:

> Law is a fabric of norms and practices in a particular society; the norms and practices are social judgments made concrete: the living, breathing embodiment of society's attitudes, prejudices, and values. Inevitably, and invariably, these are slanted in favor of the haves, the top-riders, the comfortable, respectable, well-to-do people. After all, articulate, powerful people make the laws; and even with the best will in the world, they do not feel moved to give themselves disadvantage.
>
> Rules thus tend to favor people who own property, entrepreneurs, people with good position in society. The lash of criminal justice, conversely, tends to fall on the poor, the badly dressed, the maladroit, the deviant, the misunderstood, the shiftless, the unpopular.

The *Jail Record of Grand Traverse County* gives support to Friedman's view of the law.

✦

Race or "Color," as it was expressed in the Record, was a category important to law enforcement a hundred years ago. The population of Traverse Area was not diverse; it was almost entirely white with a small representation of Native Americans and blacks. The arrest record does not support bias against those groups by the numbers. However, the few arrests of blacks were sometimes followed by immediate release the next day for a variety of reasons. This pattern may imply that blacks were arrested without cause, for simply being black in a predominantly white community. Arrests of Indians were fairly common, though it is difficult to determine if they were jailed in numbers out of proportion to their presence in the population. Whatever the true state of racism, the *Jail Record* does not directly point to bias among law enforcement.

Entries for women and children commonly appear, though in low numbers. About seven percent of arrests were women, usually for drunkenness, disorderly conduct, prostitution and larceny. Children, as young as six in one case, were admitted to the jail even less frequently. If charged at all, they were accused of truancy, larceny, or other petty crimes. It was common for such children to be sent to reformatories at Lansing or Adrian, sites of early reform schools in Michigan. One wonders at the readiness of the judge to send children away from the area for such trivial offenses. Were these reform schools simply a way to get children out of a bad situation at home or were they intended to "reform" the child morally, nipping antisocial behavior in the bud before it comes into full flower? From today's vantage point, we might question separating children from their families for committing petty offenses. In any event, the punitive purposes of present-day "adult time for adult crime" sentencing has replaced the hopes of rehabilitation that society held a hundred years ago. Progress in the juvenile justice system has not proceeded in linear fashion since that time.

※

What crimes were committed in 1900? Six hundred forty-nine of 1640 entries, nearly forty percent of all offenses, focused on drunkenness. Additionally, twenty-one cases were liquor law violations such as selling liquor out of one's house. Larceny—comprising personal theft of a bicycle, a coat at the opera house, a bicycle, as well as shoplifting—was the second most common crime with 247 cases. Assault and battery, fighting, not surprisingly appears frequently in the *Jail Record*, but domestic violence (wife beating) and rape, were scarcely mentioned. Sex-related crimes such as adultery, bigamy, prostitution, indecent exposure, and "bastardy" occur sporadically with other victimless offenses such as violations of game laws, vagrancy, and carrying concealed weapons scattered thinly throughout the book. The entries "chicken thief," "egging the teacher," "poisoned cow," and "fast driving" (in 1905) suggest a criminal population typical of a small town separated from the nefarious influences of large cities like Chicago or Detroit. All over the world people drink, break rules concerning sex, steal items, and perform all kinds of trivial antisocial acts. The people of old Traverse City were no different.

Serious crimes were recorded in the *Jail Record*, though in fairly scanty numbers. Six murders were entered between 1884 and 1902. One of these, a woman who died as a result of a "criminal operation" (probably an abortion), was downgraded to manslaughter and the physician fined one thousand dollars. Other murders had wives or lovers as victims. Apparently, at this time gunfights and physical altercations seldom resulted in death. In no way was the Grand Traverse area like the legendary "lawless West" with its shootings and revenge killings.

Robbery is mentioned eight times within the span of the book and serious assaults, both with the intent to rape or with the intent to do great bodily harm, appear sporadically. Crimes against women—rape and domestic abuse—are probably under-represented in this age before societal injustice towards women. Even within the memories of police officers still serving, complaints of domestic violence might be dealt with through mediation on site with the couple left together with the possibility of greater violence to come. Such differences between certain kinds of crimes then and now point to a change in cultural values and a change in the position of women in society.

The City of Traverse City required the Chief of Police to report arrests and detentions on a yearly basis. Between April 1, 1902 and March 31, 1903, a period that is included in the jail book's time frame, Chief Rennie reported the following information:

Arrests/Detentions	Number of Persons
Breaking bicycle ordinance	26
Assault and battery	4
False pretenses	1
Larceny	7
Drunkenness	4
Disorderly conduct	7
Lodged in lock-up until fit for release	27
Given night's lodging in city lock-up	42
Given night's lock-up in hotels	15

The table makes it clear that most of those held in jail for drunkenness were not charged with a crime, but were kept overnight until they were sober. The few that were charged with public drunkenness were probably especially troublesome to officers or the public. Some intoxicated inmates were, no doubt, put in jail for their own health and safety. Traverse City winters are unmercifully frigid and a lock-up in a warm jail cell would be preferable to possible hypothermia and death. The bottom category, "Given night's lock-up in hotels," could be designed for middle class merchants and professionals who were found drunk. Their absence from the *Jail Book* might be explained by the practice of installing them in local hotels for the night. Why this would be called a "lock-up" is unclear. Perhaps certain hotels would literally lock the doors of drinkers sobering up. The preponderance of bicycle offenses relates to a city ordinance adopted in 1900 which made many common riding behaviors criminal offenses: use of certain sidewalks for bicycling, riding faster than six miles per hour, not sounding a bell or gong upon approaching a pedestrian, night use of all city sidewalks, etc. The bicycle ordinance reflected the impact of new technology in creating a new class of offender. It would be not be the last time new machines defined new kinds of crime. The arrival of the automobile in coming decades would give rise to a vast category of traffic offenses. More recently the advancement of home computers would engender an array of internet fraud crimes. Technology, as it evolves, frequently provides new niches for lawbreakers.

✦

Comparisons between the crimes of a hundred years ago and today are difficult to make, given differences in reporting formats then and now. Within state law over the twentieth century there has been a tendency to make distinctions describing the exact nature of the crime rather than to lump all offenses under a single category. "Larceny," for example, has been divided into various subcategories which relate to the amount and kind of property that was taken. With all the changes in state law over the past century, however, it is still possible to make general statements about the reasons for arrest and incarceration at two widely separated points in history.

Another view of the jail and courthouse (Traverse Area Historical Society).

Grand Traverse County is presently studying the local criminal justice system in order to plan for possible future jail relocation and enlargement. This on-going study classifies the kinds of crimes jail inmates commit. They include domestic violence, drunk driving, traffic violations, narcotics, crimes against property, crimes against other persons, and disturbing public order. Each category accounts for a fairly large percentage of arrests, though that percentage changes over a yearly or even monthly basis. By this method of classifying crimes, how does the present pattern of arrests and detentions compare with the information given in *The Jail Record Book of Grand Traverse County*?

In examining recently collected arrest data the reader is most impressed by the fact that several categories of crime have appeared in modern times which are barely represented or not represented at all in early times. In particular, drunk driving, traffic violations, and narcotics violations do not figure in crime statistics one hundred six years ago because the automobile had not become a common feature of the landscape and because narcotics were not yet declared illegal and drug abuse was not seen to be a threat to a stable society. Furthermore, as previously discussed, in the nineteenth century domestic violence was rarely a cause for arrest since "wife-beating" generally did not merit jail time for the husband. Because violence towards women is no longer tolerated by society, the category "domestic violence" has surged in importance when compared to its paltry presence in the *Jail Record*. Here a change in societal values –the position of women in society—has resulted in a sizable increase in persons detained for violation of laws designed to protect women.

It is difficult to draw conclusions about the numbers of persons imprisoned at the dawn of the twentieth century compared to the present. Clearly more persons are caught up in the criminal justice system: jails have more cells filled with more prisoners. One reason for this rise in numbers of inmates comes from a larger County population. The 1900 census lists the population of Grand Traverse County at just over 20,000; by the year 2000 that number had increased to more than 77,000. More people mean more criminals even if the crime rate remains unchanged.

Nowadays lawbreakers are less likely to get away with their crimes. Law enforcement identifies and tracks down perpetrators through fingerprinting, increased surveillance, DNA profiling, and establishment of state and national criminal data bases. In previous times a burglar could commit a crime and flee to a neighboring state to victimize others without his record being available to law enforcement officers. Now upon arrest, fingerprint and DNA information are collected which can be used to match crime scene evidence obtained from any location within the country. Preserving anonymity is not as easy as it once was. Second, third, and successive arrests are made more readily now that criminal records are more accessible to police.

The *Jail Record of Grand Traverse County* provokes a final question: What were the beliefs of people living a hundred years ago concerning criminality? Why did people commit crimes? To a person of the nineteenth century, the answer to that question was obvious: Crime comes about through a failure in moral teaching. Arthur McDonald writes in his 1893 book, *Abnormal Man*:

> The delinquent [criminal] classes approximate nearest to the normal type [class], for the majority deviate principally in one respect, that is, in a weakness of moral sense that gives away [sic] to temptation.

Such views are not uncommon even today, though most people would not be as ready to describe criminals as members of a "criminal class." Now we recognize that crimes are committed for a variety of reasons: negligence, passion, greed, survival, and mental instability to mention only a few. MacArthur speaks of the three weakling classes: the poor, the insane, and the delinquent, lumping them together because they are dependent upon normal society for their existence. Underlying them all is a foundation of moral deficiency. The poor suffer because of intemperance and poor judgment, the insane often inherit a tendency towards mental illness from alcoholic or immoral parents, and criminals develop antisocial habits from moral neglect during their childhoods. In nearly every case, morality lay at the root of societal problems.

There is a positive aspect to this nineteenth century view of crime. Redemption, through moral instruction, is possible especially among youth. Children caught stealing or skipping school could be reformed by being sent to state reformatories. There they would be taught proper behavior and returned to their communities, thereby ending the cycle of crime parent to child. The idea of localized community care of truants, young petty thieves, and hooligans was subordinated to moral instruction carried on in large state institutions. The growth of reformatories parallels the rise of huge state-financed asylums for the mentally ill. In both cases large, state-run facilities were seen as the answer to specific social problems.

※

The *Jail Record of Grand Traverse County* lays out a script with specific roles written for criminals and law-enforcement officers. It evokes the tension between society and those who would break its rules, and in its simplicity, portrays in stark contrast the collision between two powerful forces. However, beyond this war between society and its sociopaths, there is a criminalization of ordinary human behavior: drunkenness, vagrancy, bigamy, adultery, petty larceny and the like. Those that commit such crimes are not so much disruptive of society as threatening to the prevailing social, political and religious order. In their book *The American Way of Crime*, Frank Browning and John Gerass emphasize the point:

> Control over the definition of crime and the administration of the criminal justice system has been...the dominant means by which the nation has addressed a broad range of public dilemmas. Not merely obvious crimes like murder, burglary, assault, and fraud are left to the courts, but the ever changing power relations among individuals—sex, job opportunities, family structure—are finally codified through criminal case law.

The *Jail Record*, by ignoring the misdeeds of merchants and professionals, tells us of the social control of the propertied classes over the poor. Clearly different standards were applied to deal with deviant behavior, one for the wealthy and another for those at the bottom of society. Some would argue that our present criminal code reflects similar inequalities and that enforcement of the law falls unevenly on the rich and the poor. From the vantage point of history we can look back to identify past injustice and, hopefully, to use that sharpened vision to repair the deficiencies of our own system. *The Jail Record of Grand Traverse County*, with its boldly penned entries upon dirtied pages, provides us with just such a vantage point.

CHAPTER 8

Where is the Park on Park Street?
A Study of Traverse City Street Names

Take a walk in the older parts of the city and you notice the street names: *Division* and *Union*, *Pine* and *Oak*, *Cass* and *Washington*, *Lake* and *Bay*, *Wadsworth* and *Boardman*. In general, they can be placed into four baskets: names based upon survey lines and plat maps, names based upon natural features, names based upon famous men, and names based upon local pioneers.

Division Street is located upon a section line within the Michigan Land Survey, 1851. Indeed, surveyor's records tell the names of the trees that grew along line. From the present Meijer's walking north, hemlock, white spruce and cedar come up again and again in the leather-bound books of the survey, now carefully preserved in the State Archives in Lansing Michigan. Before white settlement these trees populated the wetlands that surrounded Mill Creek (now known as Kids Creek). Now there are few of these species left, the introduced Norway spruce dominating the landscape. Still, the street names *Spruce* and *Cedar* are appropriately given, since these trees natively occupied the swampy ground beside the Creek. Similarly *Pine* and *Oak Streets* are well-named, since these trees grew upon the sandy plain that comprises most of the city. *Locust Street*,

Plat map, 1852. Note the "Park" designation for the region now occupied by the Park Place.

Traverse City, Michigan

Surveyed and Drawn 1852 by Thomas Whelpley

Of U.S. Survey

on the other hand, did not reflect original vegetation, since black locust trees were not found here before the coming of settlers. Indeed, it was named well into the twentieth century to replace *Bohemia Street* when that name became insulting to Bohemian residents because of the street's unprepossessing appearance.

Union Street, one might suppose, would connect with Civil War days, but there is no evidence that the name is related to that conflict. Since the street can be found on the first plat of the Traverse region in 1852, it predates the Civil War by some eight years. The term *Union* was not used until the outbreak of the War, so we must look elsewhere to discover the name's origin. One likely possibility stems from the Union Schools of the time, schools that draw students from two or more primary districts. While the earliest school in the area was not located on Union Street, the street could have served as a boundary between two school districts. Central High School, located only a block from Union, served as a Union School for students on both the east and west sides of the early settlement.

Then there is *Park Street*, which connects *Grandview Parkway* with *State Street* in front of the Park Place Hotel. Where is the park, you ask? In the oldest plat of the Traverse settlement, a park was clearly indicated where the hotel now stands. Perhaps the Park Place Hotel could have been named for another famous luxurious hotel, but even if it was, the name reflects the site at which it was built. An internet search under "Park Place Hotel" indicates no buildings of significant historical interest. The Traverse City building, constructed in 1929, is the oldest of them all.

Front Street, *Bay Street*, and *Lake Street* refer to geographical features of the landscape: *Front* is closest to the waterfront, *Bay* runs about the perimeter of the bay, at least part way, and *Lake* runs along the west shore of Boardman Lake. The names are straightforward, though one might wonder why *Front* is set back so far from the water. The answer is that the waterfront was crowded with docks and railroads for many years, and with the river running parallel to the shore, *Front Street* was the closest to the waterfront that was practical. In fact, the north side of the street *was* the river according to the earliest maps.

It seems that every city has a *State Street.* In Traverse City that name goes back to the original plat map, dated 1852. Perry Hannah and A. Tracy Lay, first sailed to this region from Chicago, a small town of thirty thousand people, at about that time. Already that city had its famous *State Street (...that great street...* as the song goes). Perhaps the layout of Traverse drew upon the two men's experience in Chicago. Lay spent most of his life in Chicago, while Hannah elected to live up north on the raw frontier. As Chicago grew, one wonders if Perry Hannah did not see a similar grand future for Traverse City, a future that bore small fruit within his lifetime.

Streets named after famous pioneers are found everywhere in the city. One example is *Wadsworth,* located between *Pine* and *Oak* crossing *Front Street* near the Boardman River. Abram Wadsworth (died 1871) was one of the founders of Elk Rapids. Recognized throughout the region as one the earliest settlers, Wadsworth eventually died within the Traverse settlement. Soon after, he was honored by having a street named after him.

Boardman Street was named after the river, which, in turn, was named after an early arrival, Horace Boardman, son of Harry Boardman, who purchased land at the mouth of the river in 1847. After running a sawmill for a few years, Boardman sold his land to Hannah, Lay and Co. The river and the street bear the names of men who did not commit to living in the Grand Traverse area. Other local pioneers are remembered in street names throughout the city such as Hamilton, Titus, Bates and Beadle Streets.

Cass Street was named after Lewis Cass (1782-1866), territorial governor of the Michigan Territory and, later, senator from the state of Michigan. Among the earliest named streets of town, *Cass* is the only street that honors a figure of state-wide stature. Like most cities, Traverse City commemorated national figures in its street names: *Washington, Lincoln, Webster, Franklin, Jefferson, Garfield, Monroe* and *Madison*, to name a few. Surprisingly, no presidents of the twentieth century have streets named after them within the city.

One city street is named after a foreigner. *Wellington* is named after the First Duke of Wellington (Arthur Wellesley, 1769-1852), British military leader and statesman. Known for his triumph over Napoleon at Waterloo, the Duke of Wellington also served as prime minister during the ascendancy of the British Empire. The year of his death is the exactly the same as the year the first plat map of Traverse was drawn. No doubt A. Tracy Lay and Perry Hannah, both with ancestors from the British Isles, wished to remember this Englishman by naming a street after him. The honor points to the influence of the majority of early settlers who had ethnic roots in England.

Some streets take their names after human activities: *Fair Street* ran along the old fairgrounds (now the Civic Center), and *Airport Road* was constructed in recent times as the airport moved three times in the twentieth century (from the top of Boughey Hill to *Parsons Drive* and then back to *Airport Road*). *Railroad* paralleled a railroad line, its name recalling the tracks, now torn up. Other streets take their names from natural things: *Fern* and *Rose*, for example.

More recent names reflect a trendy preoccupation with marketing or quaintness: *Quail Ridge, Cherry Lane, Coventry Trail.* As our city has become larger and more diverse, we rarely name our streets after famous people (with a few exceptions, such as Parsons Road), governors, and modern presidents. The Indian names we choose frequently do not draw upon our local Indian past: *Iroquois, Comanche, Apache Pass* represent tribes never present in Michigan. They represent a collection of names that define the boundaries of a development, an unnatural grouping of items that is unrelated to our past. Applying such names is a far cry from the naming practices of the past.

When the land was new, naming streets and roads was easier. Settlers lived on a road and it was named after them, cedar trees grew in a swamp and the nearby pathway became *Cedar Street*, all agreed that George Washington deserved to have a street named in his honor and so it was. In modern times the job of naming streets has devolved upon developers who choose names for private reasons or for the elegance a word connotes. It is a change we note, even as we remember the names of the old streets that go back before the city existed. Like arrow points, names are artifacts. As we walk and drive around our city, we should take a moment to appreciate them.

CHAPTER 9

Of Obedience, Truthfulness, and Self-Control
Dr. James Decker Munson's Views on Preventing Insanity

August 23, 1887: a fair, hot day in Traverse City. A throng of local Traverse citizens marched upstairs to the second floor lecture hall of the Ladies Library located on Front Street. Previously the *Grand Traverse Herald* announced the convening of the Sanitary Convention for the State of Michigan and invited the public, both men and women, to attend the two-day event. Lectures were on a variety of topics: Waterworks of Traverse City, Sewerage, Water Treatment, and more.

The first lecture was to be given by James D. Munson, the new head of the Northern Michigan Asylum (later, Traverse City State Hospital), on the topic "The Causes and Prevention of Insanity." A discussion was to be held following the presentation in which audience members could ask questions concerning Dr. Munson's paper. What follows is an examination of that paper with an interpretation and explanation of his view of insanity. Finally, nineteenth century perspectives on mental illness will be contrasted with present-day ideas to illuminate the different social values of the two eras.

Munson begins,

> In discussing this subject I shall be obliged to limit myself to some of the more common causes which lead to brain exhaustion, and to a few remarks concerning their prevention.

In this introductory statement Dr. Munson reveals a commonly held belief about mental illness held by most physicians in his day, namely, that insanity is caused by brain failure due to exhaustion, the weakening of brain function. Just as heart failure manifests itself in a variety of ways—shortness of breath, weakness, pain—brain failure shows a similar variety of symptoms: depression, mania, epileptic seizures, hallucinations and the like. Prevention of insanity, as we shall see later, comes from maintaining good health generally and from paying attention to good health practices that relate to brain function.

> The causes of insanity may be divided into the predisposing and the exciting. In the first group we shall find heredity, age, sex, occupation, etc. etc., and in the second all those causes "which arise from conditions in the life history of the individual," such as intemperance, domestic infelicity, ill health, overwork, and many more which need not be mentioned in this connection.

In the subsequent passage, Munson describes the importance of heredity in determining the development of mental illness. He states that sixty percent of the patients admitted to the Asylum come from "neurotic stock." The word "neurotic" here carries a different meaning from its more recent definition, which refers to a condition less severe than psychosis which includes a wide range of dysfunction: phobias, anxiety, compulsions, obsessions among others. The word "neurotic" in Munson's time referred to any disorder of the nervous system. About sixty percent of the patients reported that their families had some kind of nervous complaint. Of course, we do not know what percent of non-hospitalized people reported similar family backgrounds, a figure perhaps not much different from that calculated for the inmates. In the nineteenth century careful statistical analysis of data was rarely done, especially if doing so would jeopardize the preconceptions of the investigator.

Predisposing conditions, chief among them heredity, made individuals prone to become insane; however, with care, insanity could be avoided, providing certain good practices were followed. In the next paragraph Munson explains what parents can do to help their children avoid mental illness:

> Children should be taught the necessity of obedience and truthfulness, and above all, the necessity for self-control; and as they grow in years and in intelligence they should be admonished about certain vicious practices and taught the dangers which attend the abuse of alcoholics and narcotics.

Insanity can be brought on by a failure in moral teaching. Social control of the young is most important, since, in Munson's words, "one vicious boy may be the cause of great mischief to many others." The "vicious practices" Munson alludes to, may refer to the unlawful wildness of youth, to masturbation as well as to the explicitly mentioned "alcohol and narcotics." Not surprisingly, the emphasis on moral teaching as a means of preventing insanity is consistent with Victorian customs concerning childrearing.

Dr. Munson then quotes Douglas Yellowlees, a renowned writer on mental illness:

> Exercise, whether for duty or pleasure, implies and procures rest; and for the subject of nerve instability, sufficient and complete rest is indispensable. Rest should not be mere languid laziness, but genuine nerve repose.

Mental illness is described as a weakness in nerve function. In the nineteenth century this view gained popularity as it replaced darker notions of inherited insanity, a stain which blackened the family name forever. Not only was "nervous disease" not inherited, it also could be cured. Rest was the cure, rest combined with wholesome exercise, sometimes warm baths, and a good diet (milk diets were much in favor). Outside the asylum a number of physicians specialized in treating nervous disease through methods as diverse as hypnotism, electrical stimulation, massage, diets, and pills. As private practitioners, they were the forerunners of psychotherapists in private practice.

Yellowlees is quoted again as he proffers his opinions with regard to the emotions.

> Our emotions and affections are the mightiest factors in our lives and they afford a vast field for manifestations of nerve instability. It is in the regulation of our moral nature, and in controlling our fancies, impulses, and passions, by reason and duty, that the hardest battle must be fought.

Self-control is a key to avoiding insanity. James Munson comments,

> Many men each year lose their health by too prolonged and excessive application to business and to work.

Reason and duty impose balance to our lives. Good mental health, in turn, grows out of this balance.

Dr. Munson holds that "nerve degeneracy" does not extend through more than one or two generations. However, he laments that neurotic people tend to intermarry and that such marriages are the cause of much misery and misfortune. Despite his misgivings about such unions, he stops short of giving in to the sterilization of these couples:

> The remedy (to intermarriage among those with nervous afflictions) readily suggests itself, but as society is at present constituted not easy of practicable application. Whether certain neurotic people should marry or not is a very delicate question, the solution of which must be left to a higher civilization than ours—a civilization which will insist upon adoption of "rational principles of natural and sexual selection in the propagation of our species.

He writes here, quoting Yellowlees that our society is not yet ready to prevent "neurotics" from marrying or to sterilize them, but that such a thing may be possible in the future as society progresses. In this statement he foreshadows the coming of the eugenics movement (the notion that the unfit should be prevented from having children and that the "best" should be encouraged to reproduce) which came to flower in the twentieth centuries in America and Nazi Germany, especially).

Noting that a large percentage of Asylum patients are farmers and farmer's wives, Munson speculates that daily toil and worry about money causes mental breakdown. His advice to all those that overwork hits the mark today:

> We would say, with due respect to all toilers, introduce as much variety into life as possible; cultivate sociability, attend church, afford to yourselves and families an occasional holiday for rest and recreation; make your homes bright and cheerful, inspire your children with love and respect, and withal you will find that wealth, and all that the world most admires, will come with less anxiety, and that your health and happiness and that of your wives and children will be immeasurably increased.

Surely such ideas will never lose their currency.

Next, Dr. Munson considers the "exciting causes" of mental illness, those direct causes that trigger the onset of mental breakdown. First, it is necessary to combat the spread of contagious diseases that can bring about "fevers" which can bring about insanity.

> No epidemic sweeps the country without leaving in its train numerous mental wrecks. Little more need be said concerning these general exciting causes or their prevention. Everything that tends to promote the public health will lessen the occurrence of insanity in the commonwealth.

Certain "vicious habits," among them overactive sexuality, can lead to insanity. Here Munson is probably referring to the effects of neurosyphilis, a sexually spread condition that may result in paralysis, hallucinations and delusions, and even death. Speaking of prostitution, he says,

> Of the "social evil" is it not startling to be able to read of the existence of a modern Sodom in this year of grace? Is there a city in our proud state

> without its institutions of vice? It will suffice to say that the most fatal form of mental disease is specific in origin and the number of cases is legion.

Insanity brought on through excessive drinking was an important reason for admittance to the Asylum. It was considered especially pernicious because it led to genetic impairment in the children of the drinker.

> Intemperance not only too frequently strands its victims, but, alas, it is the father of various forms of nerve degeneracy in their offspring.

Many biologists at this time (including Munson) accepted the idea that acquired traits such as intemperance could be passed along to children by means of hereditary pathways. The sins of the fathers were indeed borne by the sons and daughters, according to this view. In fact, masturbation, deviant sexual practices including homosexuality, addictions to drugs and tobacco, as well as all kinds of immoral acts could show up in the young in the form of dementia praecox (schizophrenia) or depression or any one of a host of mental illnesses. Bad behavior causes degeneracy, and degeneracy is at the root of insanity.

Munson finishes his paper by elucidating the proper response of society to the twin evils of prostitution and intemperance:

> Primarily every effort of thinking people must continue to be exerted against them; the young must be taught their dangers, and the law must be enforced to compel those who will not listen to reason to conform to the judgment of those who have the best welfare of the human race at heart.

To prevent insanity, he says, the most important thing society can do is to educate the young about the dangers of intemperance and prostitution and to insist that moral behavior be reinforced through the law as well as other social institutions.

Discussion

The question-and-answer session that followed Dr. Munson's address touched on many topics: the general increase of the insane and the growth of the asylum system, the effects of drinking on the numbers of patients entering the asylum, the extraordinarily large proportion of foreign born inmates, Dr. Munson's philosophy of patient management, as well as the topic of women and insanity. Each question elicited remarks that helped paint a picture of the values that underlay societal values of the place and time. Munson acknowledged a general increase in the number of inmates, though he expresses his opinion that there is not an increase in insanity throughout the state. One questioner wonders if the ever larger numbers of patients is not due to the emptying of jails and poorhouses of their most distressed inmates. Drinking, while a "potent cause" of insanity, is not the sole culprit either. Most likely, the rising population of asylum inmates is due to a variety of causes; no single factor can explain it.

"Why are a solid majority of inmates foreign-born?" asks one member of the audience. Dr. Munson answers that it is possible that newly arrived immigrants are suffering the shock of pressures to succeed in their new country. Mr. Wilhelm from the audience offers his opinion, fraught with a touch of religious prejudice,

> The real reason why there is more insanity proportionally among the foreign born is that their habits at home are entirely different from what they are here. At home they work throughout the week at what they call hard work, but which in the United States would be looked upon as taking it easy, for here everything is done on the rush. On Sunday the majority of them go to church and the priest educates them to this idea, that as they do the work, he will do the thinking, which a great majority of them accept. Therefore their brains are not cultivated or strengthened. Therefore their brains are weak and can not stand much strain.

Some time is spent upon the question of the large proportion of immigrants admitted to the asylum. The issue was clearly of great importance to members of the audience. Upon re-examination of statistical data from a modern point of view, it is clear that one reason for the excessive numbers of immigrants in the asylum has to do with demographics: Immigrants tend to arrive with fewer children, and, since children are less likely to be admitted to the asylum, proportionately more of the inmates will be of non-native background. Taking demographic differences into account, the over-representation of immigrants among the patient population is largely explained.

City father Perry Hannah inquires about Dr. Munson's patient management techniques,

> I have noticed that in bringing patients to the asylum it takes two or three men to get some of them there, but after they have been in the asylum a few days they are quiet. There seems to be something in the management of the patient that quiets him. …I wish Dr. Munson would tell us the secret of his good management.

Munson replies matter-of-factly,

> After a patient is placed in the asylum, he is permitted to do much as he likes, and finding others quiet and orderly is, I think, a great incentive to him for self-control. No restraints are used and he is always treated kindly.

This simple reply speaks to us of the caring attitude Dr. Munson held towards his patients.

Finally, a note of humor creeps into Mrs. M.E.C. Bates response to the question, "What of mothers and insanity?" She says,

> The only wonder to me is that all the mothers and housekeepers are not insane. I think if we could only devise some means by which the women, like the men, could have only one thing to do instead of a hundred all at once, it would be much better.

Her reply, no doubt, is applauded by women everywhere, who offer a hearty, "Amen, sister!"

A Modern Perspective on the Causes of Insanity

No modern psychiatrist would write about the "Causes and Prevention of Insanity." Today the word "insanity" has disappeared from the medical lexicon, replaced by names of specific illnesses: Bipolar disease, Alzheimer's disease, Schizophrenia, and the like. It is not simply that the nomenclature has changed, but that the concept of "brain exhaustion" has been supplanted by a more nuanced vocabulary. Mental illness is seen as a collection of discrete, well-defined malfunctions, each, for the most part, with a definite organic cause. For a time within psychiatry, during the ascendancy of Freud, doubt was cast upon idea that mental illness was related to physical and biochemical dysfunction, but in the past twenty years most of these doubts have been put to rest. From the modern perspective, the physical failure Munson refers to does not connect with organ failure—the brain as a whole failing to function properly—but with the failure of specific signaling pathways active in identified regions of the brain. Still, his idea that something physical has gone wrong is not out of place in modern thinking.

Nor is Munson's contention that there are predisposing factors such as heredity that lead to mental illness as well as "exciting factors" (now generally lumped under the term, "stress") that can directly bring about a breakdown questioned by psychologists today. We know now that there is a hereditary predisposition to many illnesses (schizophrenia, for example), though identical twin studies do not support the dire picture Dr. Munson describes as the inescapable destiny of those with "bad genes." Many people with schizophrenic parents never develop the disease and some with no obvious hereditary predisposition are afflicted with it. The situation is not so simple as was formerly thought.

In an age before the rise of genetics, James Munson accepted the widely held view that acquired traits (such as intemperance) could result in "nerve degeneracy" in children. The sons and daughters of drunkards were at risk of mental degradation because of the missteps of the parents. Such a view has been rejected by modern science, though the social influences of growing up in a household influenced by alcoholism may result in troubled children who are at risk because of their upbringing, not their heredity. Munson's contention that the bad habits of parents can be passed along to their children (thereby debasing society) explains his yearning to prevent unfit parents from having children. In the 1880's he did not see how the state of Michigan could sterilize persons afflicted with mental illness. By the early twentieth century, however, the state had passed laws allowing for sterilization and some of these operations were performed. Within a few years however, the courts had decided that sterilization laws constituted a "cruel and unusual punishment" and were declared unconstitutional. The "higher civilization" Munson spoke of that permitted such things did not last more than a decade or two in America, though the goals of eugenics were carried forward by the Germans before and during the Second World War.

The notion that insanity can be fought through self-control carries a uniquely Victorian flavor.

> It is in the regulation of our moral nature, and in controlling our fancies, impulses, and passions, by reason and duty, that the hardest battle must be fought.

For people of the nineteenth century, morality lay at the base of every social problem. Intemperance, masturbation, homosexuality, infidelity, and rebelliousness were not just sins but pathologies that led to the mental degradation and to the asylum. The pressures placed upon individuals to behave honorably were enormous.

One pauses at Dr. Munson's reply about the management of patients.

> Restraints are not used and the patient is permitted to do pretty much what he likes.

Is an effort being made to cure the patient? Are medications used? Or are they left largely alone, letting time heal the breakdown? Given the lack of medical knowledge at the time and given the misguided practices of some asylums (e.g. some of the harsh hydrotherapy regimes), it may be a good thing the Asylum largely left people alone. By doing so, some patients might have avoided difficult life situations that brought on the onset of illness in the first place: violence at home, overwork, an unfriendly social environment, the availability of drink, etc. Perhaps, at least for some, the asylum was a place exactly as defined in the dictionary: a place of retreat and security.

CHAPTER 10

Many Wonderful Transitions
Changes in the Treatment of Mental Illness, 1885–1910

In the early years of the Northern Michigan Asylum, the board of trustees of the hospital was required to send a report to Lansing which would describe the operation of the institution as well as provide a budget designed to account for how state money was being spent in the care of the insane. The report was prepared by James Decker Munson, the first superintendent of the asylum, every other year until 1919, after which other reporting methods were employed. Dr. Munson's report of 1910 is especially illuminating, since it provides a summary of changes in the mental health field over the previous twenty-five year period as seen through the superintendent's eyes. The purpose of this chapter is to examine this report from a historical perspective in order to understand the ideas that guided the treatment of mental illness in the late nineteenth and early twentieth centuries. In the following paragraphs, the words of Dr. Munson will alternate with commentary by the author.

It would be difficult to fully compare the conditions surrounding the insane twenty-five years ago with those of today. Previous to that time the insane were mostly cared for in county-houses, some—the more violent—

were locked in jails, some were kept at home in various sorts of receptacles, and asylum care was minimized to save expense. Restraints, both chemical and mechanical, were largely used; trained nursing was unknown, and very little if any care was given patients at night. During these early years every effort was bent to improve the housing, feeding and nursing of this class of sick people. Gradually county care gave way to asylum care and finally state care for the insane was established since which time wonderful changes for the better have taken place in all these things.

The asylum, especially in the early part of the nineteenth century was regarded as a social innovation designed to offer care to people suffering from mental illness. Dr. Munson's description of care before the asylum era is accurate. Frequently, families were ashamed of their insane relatives and kept them at home, often locked away from others. If emotional and financial pressures were too great, troubled family members would be abandoned at county-funded facilities that made no effort to treat inmates (it would be incorrect to call them "patients") who suffered afflictions as diverse as schizophrenia, depression, and general paresis (the condition later identified as an outcome of neurosyphilis). Many thousands of the mentally ill were incarcerated in jails or simply allowed to wander around the countryside. It was a time before the social safety net had been constructed.

During the last twenty-five years many wonderful transitions have occurred in almost every department of human effort. Our knowledge of diseased mental states and their treatment, of mental hygiene, and of applied or practical psychology, have almost wholly developed within that time. The psychic laboratory; the psycho-analysis of Freude [sic] and Jung; the clinical methods of Kraepelin and his pupils—unused and unknown till a few years ago—are of immense value to the mental and nervous sufferer. Psychology is making rapid progress and applied psychology is used by the business man as well as by the teacher and physician. It is of great value in the examination of school children of railway employees, and in the examination and treatment of many morbid nervous and mental states.

A lithograph of the Northern Michigan Asylum made in 1886. (Traverse Area Historical Society)

Munson's statement affirming the advance of knowledge about diseased mental states gives the reader pause. Medical research had revealed little about the physical causes of insanity and had not suggested effective treatments for most illnesses. The spirochetes of syphilis were not positively identified as the cause of general paralysis until 1916. Pellagra, with its neuropsychiatric symptoms, was not understood as a vitamin deficiency disease until 1926. In this 1910 report to Lansing, Munson was optimistic in his assessment of scientific knowledge into mental disease.

The term 'mental hygiene' had taken on a specific meaning by 1910. It referred to insanity as a public health problem, and not simply the product of improper individual behavior. The mental hygiene movement, which became popular in the early years of the nineteenth century, was regarded as a scientific approach to controlling insanity. It emphasized education, prevention of disease related to mental illness, temperance, care of the feebleminded, eugenics, management of abnormal children, as well as the prevention of crime and prostitution. Where nineteenth century notions of preventing insanity asserted patients acquired disease through heredity and lapses in moral decision-making, the mental hygiene movement added a third element: an unhealthy environment that society could improve through community effort. The onus placed upon individuals for their illness had slipped off their shoulders slightly. Now society itself would have to accept some responsibility for the prevention of mental disease.

Within the state of Michigan, the psychic laboratory Munson alludes to refers to the Psychopathic Hospital associated with the University of Michigan, founded in 1906. There patients were examined and diagnosed before being sent to Kalamazoo, Pontiac, Traverse City, or Newberry. The psychic laboratory in Ann Arbor could help asylum physicians diagnose puzzling cases, or provide autopsies for patients who died in the asylum. To James Decker Munson, it represented a scientific, medical approach to patient admissions and care. After all, Ann Arbor was closer to the world of cutting-edge science than Traverse City.

Munson's mention of Freud and Jung in 1910 indicates his interest in European developments in the field of psychology. Neither Freud nor Jung aimed their therapies at asylum patients; they concentrated on Northern European upper middle-class women, often Jewish, who were afflicted with neurasthenia, depression, and anxiety. The ratio of doctors to patients was too high in asylums to enable caregivers to offer the long conversations about intimate subjects required in psychoanalysis. Besides, such therapy had never been shown to be effective in treating dementia praecox (schizophrenia), mania, catatonia, and a host of other mental diseases. In mentioning Freud, Munson is talking about the impact of new ideas on society generally, not about changes in the treatment of patients in the asylum.

The clinical methods of Kraepelin and his students marked a change in how mental illness was classified. Formerly—and Munson's earlier reports to the state confirm this—insanity was classified according to a scheme modified from that of Krafft-Ebing. In this system, *degeneracy* was regarded as a salient feature of any mental illness. That is, insanity results from hereditary weakness that is passed from parents to offspring. Furthermore, moral failure such as a propensity towards alcoholism, could be passed on to children, sometimes changing from one form to another. A case of intemperance in a parent, for example, could display itself as mania in a son or daughter.

By 1910 serious questions were being asked by scientists concerning the inheritance of acquired traits within biology, but conclusive proof against the theory was lacking. (In fact, it was not until the 1950's that the last arguments in favor of the inheritance of acquired traits were overturned) Psychiatrists like James Decker Munson were not out of step with scientific thinking of the time in believing an acquired trait like alcoholism could be passed along to children. He, along with the majority of his peers, would collect detailed information about each patient's background: hospitalizations for mental illness, intemperance, senility, suicides, melancholia, and even shattered marriages. The purpose of such inquiries was to determine the likelihood of recovery. Insanity of the degenerate kind was rarely curable.

Kraepelin, from 1896, rejected the older notion of degeneracy. His approach was to collect information about patients with a view towards understanding the course of the disease and its prognosis: Would they recover or not? Upon examination of descriptions of his patients' symptoms, he divided psychiatric illness into two main categories: those with an affective component and those without. The word 'affect' refers to mood;

diseases such as mania, depression, manic-depression (a term created by Kraepelin), and anxiety were placed together because they shared an emotional component. Many of these illnesses would respond to treatment or would get better on their own. Opposed to these illnesses were those conditions that did not involve the emotions; the most important of them was dementia praecox (or, as it came to be known, schizophrenia). The prognosis was poor for this group; most would not get better. In adopting Kraepelin's classification of insanity, James Decker Munson was a man forced to reject elements of his early education in psychiatry. Trained in theories of degeneracy, he changed his thinking as new ideas penetrated psychiatry. It is to his credit that he retained this flexibility into his old age.

Munson's aside about the advance of applied psychology especially as it relates to business and education may relate to the advent of vocational aptitude testing and counseling. Early in the twentieth century counselors in schools informed students about different vocations and had begun testing them to sort out those destined for college from those predisposed for the trades and manual labor. By 1908 Frank Parsons had founded the Boston Vocational Bureau, a service designed to help young people identify a future career for themselves. Businesses also used vocational aptitude tests to sort out the most promising candidates for jobs. It is unlikely that Munson was referring to general intelligence testing, since the popular Stanford Simon-Binet IQ test was not developed until 1916. By 1917 all recruits into the army were given intelligence tests, beginning an era of IQ testing which has still to play itself out. In 1910, the year Munson prepared his report to Lansing concerning the Northern Michigan Asylum, such testing was seldom performed.

After a short paragraph concerning advances in brain surgery (advances, which, in retrospect seem insignificant), Munson speaks optimistically of a future decline in asylum admissions.

> We are hopeful that insanity and all forms of degeneracy will be greatly lessened in the next generation. We are just beginning to recognize in this state the benefit of state care. The increase of cases has been comparatively small during the last four years, and there has been a noticeable

> decrease in the insane population of the hospital during the last year. If senile patients were excluded from admission to the hospital, as was the practice 25 years ago, we believe there would be a marked decrease in the average number of occurring cases per year in the state.

Edward Shorter in his book *A History of Psychiatry* describes the growth of the elderly insane population in England and the United States during the twentieth century. James Munson's observation that senile patients made up an increasingly large proportion of hospital admissions is consistent with national and international trends. As far as Traverse City's asylum was concerned, senile patients continued to be admitted in large numbers until the middle of the twentieth century. For this reason, any hope for a reduction in patient numbers was shattered for many years beyond Munson's tenure as superintendent.

Dr. Munson spends many words describing the beauty of the asylum's campus as well as detailing the efficiencies of the farm.

> A lake was constructed in the center of the grounds in front of the institution and makes a pretty feature of the asylum park. It is surrounded by rare trees, shrubs, and flowers, and is a favorite spot for women patients. The high and wooded grounds back of the asylum are also very beautiful, and with their hills, dales, and valleys, rivulets, roadways, and pathways, are almost ideal for the recreation of the nervous invalid.

This description reminds us of the words of Thomas Kirkbride, dating from the 1830's. Like that towering figure from the early days of the asylum movement, Munson expresses the healing power that resides in the beauty of nature. Sounding as relics of a nearly forgotten age, his thoughts contrast with his earlier praise of the advance of medicine and psychoanalytic treatment. Nature still has its curative powers, even if they cannot be documented scientifically.

> Psychiatric knowledge has developed very rapidly during the last few years, and while much light has been thrown on many difficult mental

problems, still more difficult ones of solution seem to loom up as greater knowledge of nervous functions is gained. Great advances have been made in our knowledge of the etiology and treatment of psychoneuroses, in the methods of psycho-analysis of Freude and Jung and Putman and Prince and others. The subjects of heredity and especially of environment, are more justly appreciated and studied than ever before, and brain surgery, and the physiology and chemistry of the internal secretions, have wonderfully advanced in practical importance. The discovery of the sero-diagnosis of lues, and the widening field of organotherapy, and the vaccine treatment of certain diseases, are among the most remarkable and valuable of recent medical achievements.

The psychoanalysis methods of Freud, in retrospect, represented a mistaken pathway for psychiatry generally, but other advances in medicine did result in improved treatment for the insane. The "sero-diagnosis of lues (syphilis)" was such an advancement, since neurosyphilis was a significant problem in early twentieth century America. Though the medicine Salvarsan was discovered in 1908 as a cure for syphilis, its side effects were pernicious. A positive diagnosis of syphilis without resorting to microscopic examination of tissues was a step forward, as Munson noted.

Organotherapy—the use of secretions obtained from glands and organs of the body—had made an important contribution to bettering the physical and mental health of the world's people. For example, it was discovered that myxedema, a condition in which victims sometimes showed mental deterioration, could be treated by extracts from the thyroid gland, taken either by injection or orally. In addition, promising experiments had been done with regard to the injection of pancreatic solutions in an effort to treat diabetes. In 1910, however, diabetes was still poorly understood. Patients would have to wait for several more decades before insulin administration would become widespread.

Fevers, as they were called at this time, sometimes did result in insanity and preventative measures might reduce asylum populations, though in very small numbers. By 1910 vaccines for rabies, anthrax, and typhoid had been developed with more to come in the twenties. Prevention of disease meant fewer patients admitted to mental hospitals with brains damaged from microorganisms. Indeed, it was an advance that helped a small fraction of hospital patients.

Dr. Munson ends his report on an optimistic note. He notes the educational campaigns of public schools in teaching

> ...the evil effects of, direct and remote, of the improper use, or abuse, of alcoholics, tobacco and other drugs, and of bad or imperfect personal hygiene and sanitary surroundings, including want and privation, malnutrition and bodily diseases which hinder normal soul development, has been of vast importance.

He goes on to acknowledge the responsibility of the state in insuring that children are brought up properly, even referring to it as a "Spartan ideal" which has been revived (though assuring his audience that no sacred right of the family will be interfered with). It is a clear exposition of the mental hygiene movement, a force which exerted much influence in the early years of the twentieth century.

On a broad scale society can adopt measures to prevent insanity. However, it is scientific progress that will provide therapy if not a cure. The psychopathic hospital in Ann Arbor receives praise from Munson for its skills in diagnosis of new patients as well as diagnosis of deceased patients, the autopsies aiding physicians in understanding underlying pathologies. A commonly agreed upon system of classification of mental illnesses was another recent achievement of the state of Michigan. Such a nosology enabled all asylums to use the same reporting procedures. From the tone of Dr. Munson's report, a bright future lay before the mental health community.

Such an attitude carries over from the optimism that pervaded medicine generally in the early twentieth century. The germ theory of disease was a major breakthrough and vaccination, diet changes among the population, improved sanitary practices, and other public health practices were bringing about positive outcomes in preventing disease and lowering mortality generally. Though medicine made enormous strides forward after the turn of the century, psychiatry would have to wait fifty more years for its quantum leap forward into the modern age of treatment. That leap was the discovery of neuroleptic drugs, chlorpromazine and reserpine, medicines that proved effective in treating schizophrenia and bipolar disease. Dr. Munson's optimism did not prove false in the long run; it simply took more time than he might have guessed before society could enjoy the benefits of the scientific advances he awaited so eagerly.

⁕

James Decker Munson represented a bridge between the nineteenth and twentieth centuries. In 1910 he still uses the word 'degeneracy' in his biennial report. At the same time, he speaks of the responsibility of society to provide an environment conducive to good mental health, a view not consistent with mainstream thinking twenty-five years before. Freud and Jung appear in this paper, foreshadowing their influence in years to come. However, taking a position in opposition to psychoanalysis, Munson indicates that mental illness results from physical dysfunction, an understanding that would have to be rediscovered in mid-century. Reaching back to the beginning years of the asylum movement, he describes the physical beauty of the Northern Michigan Asylum, a place where "the nervous invalid" may find a refuge, a place for recreation. After a description of the gardens, ponds, forests and meadows, he returns to scientific diagnosis of mental disease. Always there is a back-and-forth exchange of nineteenth century and twentieth century ideas. In later decades of the twentieth century, other superintendents would reach a modern understanding of patient treatment. However in the end, through his openness to new ideas, James Decker Munson brought the Traverse City State Hospital into the modern age. For this among many reasons, we should pay him honor.

CHAPTER 11

What Do Old Textbooks Tell Us of the Past?
The Values Taught at School a Hundred Years Ago

An elementary school textbook writes, "But when Uncle Sam set his left foot on the Hawaiian Islands, in the Central coast of Asia, these powers of Europe opened their eyes and began to get new ideas about the great republic of the West. It was plain that the United States had become a world power, and that when the game of empire was to be played, the western colossus must be asked to take a hand." A book of Advanced Geography says this: "[White people] are the most active, enterprising, and imaginative race of the world; they speak many languages and are divided into many nations." A biology textbook from the nineteen thirties informs us: "In certain of the classes of idiots, feeble-minded, and insane, the defects can be inherited. Entrance of one feeble-minded person into the country may result in a few generations of the production of several hundred individuals with the same defect."

Such questions speak of a different world from that we now inhabit, yet they were made in a social context that made sense at the time. Our grandfathers and grandmothers learned much that we would question today, but still we cling to the vestiges of that teaching through casual statements passed down through families. It is important to look at what we believed three or four generations ago to cast a light on the truths that governed lives then. In doing so, we can understand our own lives now.

Eugenics as Taught in High School Textbooks of the Early Twentieth Century

Science is often said to be "objective" or "values-neutral." That is, it does not depend upon societal ideas of right and wrong, good and bad, but touches directly on objective truth. In fact, as explained by Stephen Jay Gould, late professor of Evolutionary Biology at Harvard University, in the past science has often been connected to societal values in the questions it seeks to answer, in the methods it employs, in the means by which it is funded, and in the way ideas are accepted, promoted, and published both inside and outside a particular branch of science. That is not to say science is just another point of view. Science is undeniable truth that applies equally to all people. That the Earth revolves about the sun is not simply a belief but a fact. Differences in culture cannot change it. At the same time, the mantle of authority of science has been borrowed by people who wish to promote their own definition of morality. Science confers respectability upon a subject. A good example is eugenics, an area of scientific inquiry that was popular during the period between the two World Wars.

Eugenics was an outgrowth of advances in genetics following the rediscovery of Mendel in the year 1900. A commonly used high school Biology text used at the time, *A Civic Biology,* defines it this way: *Eugenics is the science of being well born.* This enigmatic definition is fleshed out in the telling of the Jukes and the Kallikaks, families with grave genetic shortcomings that passed on those traits for generations. *A Civic Biology* describes the sorry pedigree of the Kallikaks family thus:

> This family has been traced to the union of Martin Kallikak, a young soldier of the War of the Revolution, with a feeble-minded girl. She had a feeble-minded son from whom there have been to the present time 480 descendents. Of these 33 were sexually immoral, 24 confirmed drunkards,

> 3 epileptics, and 143 feeble-minded. The man who started this terrible line of immorality and feeble-mindedness later married a normal Quaker girl. From this couple a line of 496 descendents have come with no cases of feeble-mindedness. The evidence and the moral speak for themselves!

The point of eugenics is clear: mental and moral defects are inherited and that humans must improve their genetic stock just as they would the animals they breed.

Stephen Jay Gould examines the Kallikak study from a modern point of view. Though IQ testing had been invented some years before the study, it was not employed in determining the intelligence of the progeny of Martin Kallikak. Instead, the author of the investigation, H.H. Goddard, employed a woman, Ms. Kite, who possessed an uncanny ability to determine intellectual capacity and moral fitness from photographs and from oral testimony. Of course there was no scientific validity to the study, though its conclusions were published widely in school textbooks throughout the first half of the century. By 1928 Goddard admitted that he was mistaken concerning the heritability of intelligence. Still, his Kallikak study was quoted in textbooks published as recently as the nineteen-thirties.

A Civic Biology does not stop with describing the "problem." It goes on to suggest remedies to the dilution of "good" genes by the "bad."

> If such people [as the Kallikaks] were lower animals, we would probably kill them off to prevent them from spreading. Humanity will not allow this, but we do have the remedy of separating the sexes in asylums or other places and in various ways preventing intermarriage and the possibilities of perpetuating such a low and degenerate race. Remedies of this sort have been tried successfully in Europe and are now meeting with success in this country.

The dark reference to Europe foreshadows the triumph of Hitler's racial cleansing policies of the thirties and forties.

ATTITUDES TOWARDS RACE AS EXPRESSED IN GEOGRAPHY BOOKS

Dodge's Advanced Geography (Michigan Edition) was intended for use by students of the middle grades, an observation supported by the author's confession that the questions and exercises at the end of the chapters were prepared by Miss Caroline W. Hotchkiss, a teacher of seventh grade geography. Published in 1904, it is a large and handsome book with many photographs and colored maps. Since most students at this time would stay in school through the eighth grade, the lessons learned here went out to the young of all social classes—future college presidents as well as laborers. For young adolescents, the curriculum is largely the same no matter the background of the families of the students served.

What did they learn about humanity? For one thing they learned that civilizations can be ranked on a linear scale.

> The lowliest people are those who get their living entirely by hunting and fishing or by digging edible roots, or by gathering the fruits of plants that grow around them. These people we call *savage*.

Ranking above these poor souls, are barbarous people, those that practice primitive agriculture and herding. Above both are civilized people, those who create wealth by breaking down work into specific jobs rather than having one person do it all. Sadly, the natives of Australia are the least civilized people in the world, subsisting on the animals they hunt and the plants they gather. Even the industrious Chinese are not given credit for the accomplishments of their ancient civilization.

> As a rule they (the Yellow Race) include some of the most backward tribes of the world.

Evidently the author of this text, Richard Elwood Dodge, was unaware of the enormous advancements made by Chinese civilization over the course of the last two millennia. For much of recorded history, in fact, the civilization of China was far ahead of that of Europe.

The section of *Dodge's Advanced Geography* that deals with racial descriptions has humankind divided into four races: white, yellow, red, and black. The order is intentional. It proceeds from the highest to the lowest. In using colors to separate races, Dodge is following an old tradition. Carolus Linnaeus, the founder of modern biological classification, in the eighteenth century described the races of man using one main characteristic, geography, and three lesser ones: color, temperament, and posture. The colors, of course, do not mirror the true colors of human beings, but they were, in the judgment of scholars of the time, "close enough." Temperament originally referred to the four humors of the body: phlegm (sluggishness), blood (activity), choler (anger), and melancholy. Vestiges of Linnaeus's racial classification are retained in the textbook description by the author's insistence that whites were "active, enterprising, and imaginative" while blacks were "somewhat indolent like other peoples whose homes are in tropical countries." Posture, the last of Linnaeus's characteristics, had to do with stature, height as compared to whites. It was noted that the Yellow race was shorter than the others.

The racism of early textbooks was not questioned by scholars or teachers at the time of their use. White supremacy had a long history in Europe and was brought here with the colonists. While a few brave souls, both black and white—Whitman, Thoreau, W.E.B. Dubois, and Fredrick Douglas—would speak out against racial prejudice and intolerance in the nineteenth century, it would take many decades before such attitudes would be confronted by the American people. Indeed, that confrontation continues today.

American Triumphalism as Illustrated by an Early Textbook

Charles Morris in his elementary textbook *Pictorial History of the United States* writes in his introduction

> Just think of it! All that we see around us is the work of less than three hundred years! No doubt many of you have read in fairy tales of wonderful things done by the Genii of the East, of palaces built in a night, of cities moved miles away from their sites. But here is a thing as wonderful and at the same time true, a marvel wrought by men instead of magical beings. These great forests have fallen, these great fields have been cleared and planted, these great cities have risen, these myriads of white men have

taken the place of the red men of the wild woods, and all within a period not longer than three times the life of the oldest men now living. Is not this as wonderful as the most marvelous fairy tale?

The book is a celebration of America. Americans are good. The changes they have brought about are good. The wilderness has been tamed and the spread of civilization is like a fairy tale in its power and its fascination. The optimism of the nineteenth century fairly jumps out from the pages.

In reading the passage today we step back a moment to ponder the meanings rather than wholeheartedly joining Morris in his celebration.

The great forests have fallen, these great cities have risen, these myriads of white men have taken the place of the red men of the wild woods—

Here is something that holds us back from rejoicing. Is it a quiet lamentation for the great forests that have fallen, a regret especially strong in those of us from the white pine country of Northern Michigan? Is it the sordidness of our great cities that stretch out in miles of dirty asphalt? Or, is it the sour note of injustice as we note the eviction of the Indians from their lands? Something holds us back, a hundred years after this textbook was studied in schools.

The pride Charles Morris took in the logging of forests was a reflection of that of Thomas Jefferson who envisioned the future United States as a vast acreage of small farms and villages, each occupied by freedom-loving men and women. It is not surprising Jefferson and so many of his compatriots looked forward to the end of wilderness. After all, many of them had connections with Europe, a place from which wilderness had long ago disappeared. From their perspective civilization was not compatible with wilderness. The forests, the swamps, the uncharted lands of the West were an affront to modern ways.

In nineteenth century America the rise of cities was akin to the fruiting of mushrooms after a rain. Chicago was a small town of 30,000 in 1850. There were no towns of north of Grand Rapids with a population greater than 2000 at this time. "Great cities" were few: New York, Philadelphia, Boston and a few others. Still, by 1900, especially in contrast to the old cities of Europe, American cities had already achieved growing populations that pointed to future growth. The optimism of the people made sense in view of the entrance of the United States onto the world stage through its population increase, its conversion of wilderness to farmland, the growing wealth of its industries, and, with the advent of the Spanish-American War, its movement towards building an empire.

The defeat of the "red man" was justified in various ways. *A Pictorial History of the United States* makes a weak argument stating that the Indians did not need so much land to survive:

> Some people say there are as many of them as there ever were. If that is so, they can live on much less land than they once occupied.

Another justification was that the Indians behaved abominably towards each other so that the wars against the white man did not add appreciably to the sum-total of savage behavior.

> People say that they were badly treated by the whites, but they treated one another worse than the whites ever did.

Furthermore, killing them and driving them from their lands served a greater good: the tranquility to come.

> No doubt the white men have treated them very unjustly, but they have stopped all these terrible cruelties [towards each other and whites] and that is something to be thankful for. In this country, where once there was constant war and bloodshed, and torturing and burning of prisoners, now there is peace and kindness and happiness. So if evil has been done, good has come of it.

That the author of a children's textbook should take so much space to rationalize the whites' treatment of the Indians indicates the unease many felt about genocides, the Trail of Tears, and the appropriation of tribal lands perpetrated by the ruling class.

Textbooks Codify Our Beliefs and Attitudes

History is not a collection of facts about the past. Biology is not always an objective description of the ways of living things. Both subjects, as presented in school curriculum, necessarily leave out certain ideas and emphasize others. Furthermore, they use language that is freighted with hidden meanings. A child's history of the United States published in 1901 did not discuss the injustices of the Mexican-American War, the abuses of industrialists towards their workers, the Suffragette movement, or the period of Reconstruction in the South. On the other hand, four chapters are devoted to the conduct of the Revolutionary War with a separate biographical chapter on George Washington. Science, too, was not immune from value-laden choices made by authors with strong political and social views. As we have seen, the inclusion of eugenics as a topic in high school biology, even though based upon poor science, helped spread ideas that supported the sterilization of "defectives" in asylums in this country and, later, in Nazi Europe. Similarly, a pseudo-scientific treatment of race reinforced white supremacy attitudes and degraded the achievements and abilities of other peoples of the world.

All of this would not be important if ideas stayed locked in the towers of academia. They do not. Through the school curriculum ideas are spread among those least equipped to question them: the young. Students are required to learn the stuff of textbooks. Furthermore, the material they had to learn was often taught by teachers with little understanding of history and science. Questioning the conclusions of textbooks was not encouraged at the dawn of the twentieth century; rather, memorization and obedience were demanded. In the social context of schools, the history curriculum *was* history and the science curriculum *was* science. Not surprisingly, the racism that has plagued our nation from the earliest times has been propagated in school curriculum throughout our past. By acknowledging that fact we can open ourselves to the possibility of change.

⁘

Note: The textbooks examined here were not necessarily used in the Traverse City School District, but they could have been. *A Civic Biology* was an important biology text published in 1914. Interestingly, it was the text John Scopes taught out of in the Scopes "Monkey Trial" of 1923. I have examined many biology books of the era and discovered most, if not all, had a chapter on eugenics. *Dodge's Advanced Geography* also may not have been used here. That it had a Michigan edition implies that it sold many copies within the state, however. Similarly Morris's *Pictorial History of the United States* may not have been used locally. Its ideas, however, were common to most U.S. history texts of the time.

The Hannah-Lay sawmill near the mouth of the Boardman River, taken about 1869. (Traverse Area Historical Society)

CHAPTER 12

How We Changed the Lake
Tracing the Impacts of Settlement on Grand Traverse Bay and Lake Michigan

In middle of the nineteenth century the primitive settlement of Traverse City had a steam-powered sawmill at the mouth of the Boardman River. Where horizontal juniper and bearberry stretched out their stems just back from the water's edge a few years before, now stood a black engine that powered the saws that cut the white pine into clean, white boards stacked in neat piles awaiting transportation to Chicago and beyond. The smoke from the stack, the ash produced by the boiler fire, the slabs of bark, and the sawdust produced by the screaming saws were an assault upon the Bay's water and its fishes. It was the beginning of a long and sorry history that marked the decline of a vigorous fresh-water ecosystem that had stood intact for thousands of years before white settlement. At times painful to tell, the story helps us understand the changes that ecosystem experienced as well as the changes in the way people came to view the Great Lakes.

Upstream a mile from the sawmill, Boardman Lake spread out its waters, seemingly the result of an impoundment of the river, but actually a natural lake of respectable depth. It was here in the winter of 1859 local Indians were seen practicing their means of ice fishing. Morgan Bates, the editor of the region's first newspaper, *The Grand Traverse Herald*, provides us with a description:

> The Indians are now engaged in fishing for them [lake trout]. They cut a hole through the ice, cover it with evergreen boughs, throw in an artificial decoy fish attached to a line, throw themselves flat upon their faces, and, with spear in hand, watch the approach of the unsuspecting trout to the decoy, when, quick as lightning, the spear is thrust, and a ten or twenty pound trout is floundering on the ice.[1]

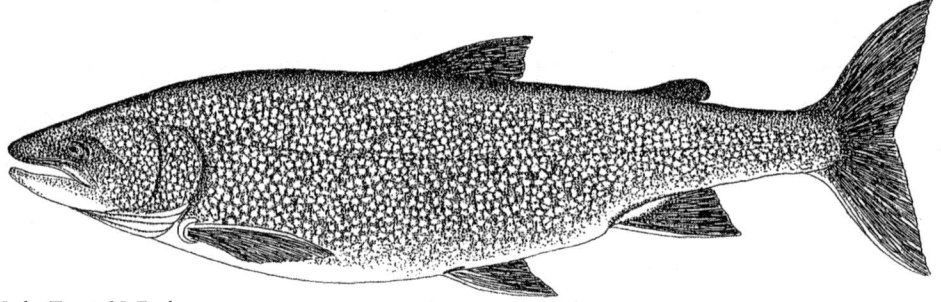

Lake Trout, N. Fogle

Bate's description of ten to twenty pound lake trout was not a fisherman's exaggeration. Before 1850 when large-scale commercial fishing began in earnest, the Great Lakes had tremendous populations of whitefish, lake trout, and sturgeon with individuals much larger than their counterparts taken today.[2] A reliable report from Mackinac Island tells of an eighty pound lake trout taken in nearby waters. Sturgeon were common at the time; one estimate puts their numbers at over eleven million over the Great Lakes ecosystem.[3] They, too, were enormous. A note in the 1869 *Herald* tells of a fifty-one pounder speared in the Boardman River and, in the following issue, another from the Platt River measuring nearly six feet in length and weighing seventy-seven pounds[4]. It was to be the last hurrah of this curious fish. The next fifty years would bring it close to extinction within the Great Lakes.

Sturgeon, N. Fogle

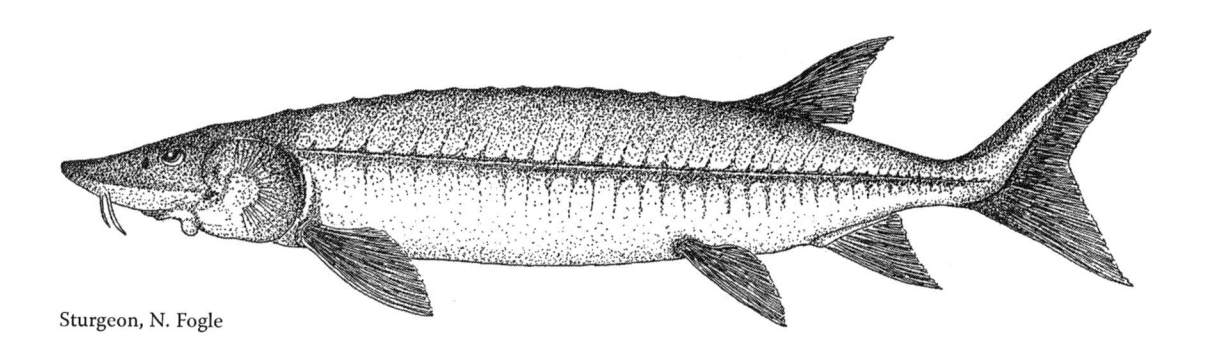

At first sturgeon were regarded as a trash fish. With bony scales covering part of its body, a pointed snout and downward facing mouth, feelers, and a shark-like tail, they did not look like other fish. Furthermore, their meat tasted bad—so people said—and they had a reputation for eating fish eggs of more desirable species. Consequently, they were speared, netted, burned, left ashore to rot—despised not just for their ugly looks but for their uselessness. Since merely being in the way of human activity is not as risky as being the object of human desire, they might have survived such treatment. But it was not to be, for sturgeon was found to have value after all.

First, it tasted—well, not so bad after all, especially if the meat was smoked. And then, a fine caviar could be made from its eggs. Furthermore, its swim bladder yielded a clear liquid that could be used in making isinglass, not the isinglass made of mica but that used as a clear adhesive. The value of sturgeon shot upwards during the last two decades of the nineteenth century, and as it did, the numbers of the fish brought to market peaked in 1892. The recovery to prior population levels never occurred. No doubt the fifteen to twenty-five years required for it to reach sexual maturity had something to do with it. Perhaps, too, logging operations and sawmills with their attendant sawdust pollution spoiled their breeding areas at river mouths and upstream. Whatever the reason, the fish is no longer found in the Boardman River.

As with sturgeon, whitefish diminished in size and numbers as commercial fishing expanded.[5] Unlike sturgeon, there was never doubt about the value of the species.

Great Lakes Whitefish, N. Fogle

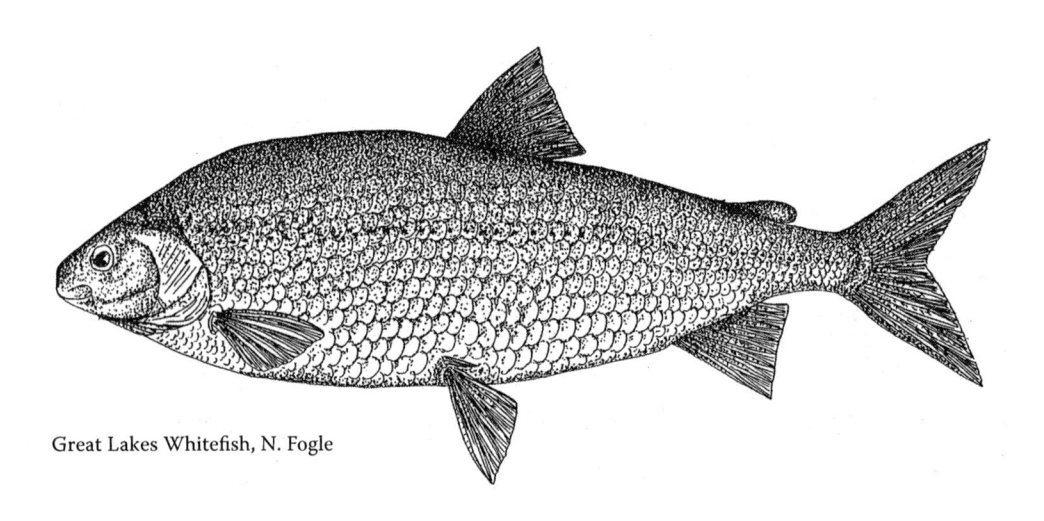

It was delicious. The plundering of this resource took place with breath-taking rapidity. Between 1879 and 1899 the commercial catch went from 24 million to 9 million pounds. At the peak of production, Great Lakes whitefish was sold all over the United States and even as far as Liverpool, England all year around at a reasonable price. Of course, it could not last. Not only was overfishing wiping out the species but spawning areas were being destroyed as dams and logging operations filled in shallow, sandy areas with silt and sawdust. Like salmon, at least some whitefish migrated upstream to spawn. With dams blocking their way, their usual mating habits were disrupted. There was no way they could replace the numbers that were being taken by the nets of the fishermen. Whitefish, while still occupying an important place in the Great Lakes fishery, never returned to its place of prominence as a source of food for local residents.

The dams, sawmills, and logging operations that damaged whitefish spawning areas also affected a fish of local rivers: the grayling. Preferring cold streams of the subarctic, this species inhabited several river systems of northern lower Michigan including the Muskegon, Manistee, Jordan, and AuSable (though probably not the Boardman).[6] Building dams, removing shade trees, rolling logs down steep banks as well as the battering traffic of the logs themselves destroyed the gravel areas upon which the fish laid

Mackinac fishing boats (Traverse Area Historical Society)

their eggs. Predation by stocked brook trout as well as unregulated fishing contributed to its demise, too. By the first decade of the twentieth century it had largely disappeared from the lower peninsula, a victim incapable of coping with Western industry and civilization.[7]

The Arrival of New Species

The impacts of habitat destruction and overfishing on the fishery were in some ways dwarfed by the introduction of new species into the Great Lakes ecosystem.[8] The opening of the St. Lawrence Seaway in 1933 provided a pathway for two species that forever changed the upper Great Lakes: the sea lamprey and the alewife. Both entered the upper four Lakes (Erie, Huron, Michigan, Superior) by means of the Welland Canal, the waterway that enabled them to get around Niagara Falls. By the nineteen thirties the lamprey had reached the waters of Northern Lake Michigan with the alewife not far behind.[9] Their arrival had a cataclysmic effect on the Lakes.

The sea lamprey brought about the near demise of the ecosystem's top predator, the lake trout. As a result of lamprey parasitism (and overfishing), lake trout numbers plummeted and, by the 1940's, natural reproduction was infrequent. With diminished numbers of lake trout and other predatory species, alewife populations surged, resulting in periodic massive die-offs that covered sandy beaches with piles of rotting fish. By the 1960's the situation was intolerable. A suitable predator had to be introduced into the Lakes.

And it was. Coho and Chinook salmon were introduced to the Great Lakes by the state of Michigan in 1966-67. They performed admirably, consuming vast quantities

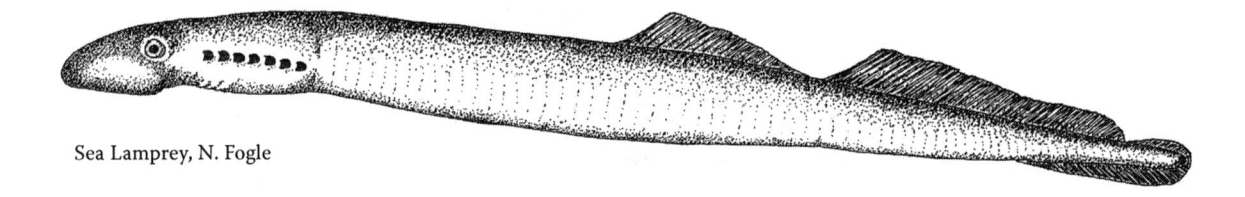

Sea Lamprey, N. Fogle

of alewives as well as providing the basis for a strong sport fishery. Since little natural reproduction occurred, fingerlings were planted yearly to maintain populations.

The fish are harvested for a variety of purposes—human consumption, caviar, and pet food. Despite these benefits, onshore salmon fishing bothers those fishermen with early trout fishing experience they hold as a treasured memory. The crowded riverbanks with dead and rotting carcasses on sandy shoals are not what they associate with their sport.

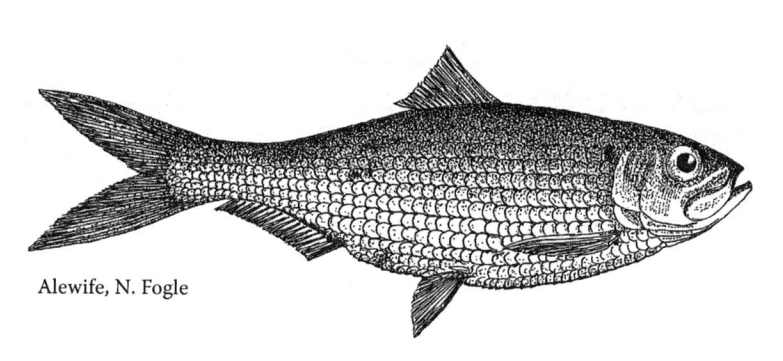

Alewife, N. Fogle

Rainbow smelt was another introduction that claimed a mixed reputation. First planted in Crystal Lake in 1912, the species spread rapidly throughout the Lake Michigan and Huron basin. Spectacular smelt runs occurred in early spring and smelt dipping became a sport of many. Still, there was a downside to this introduction. Did it eat the young of desirable species such as perch? What species were losing out as smelt prospered? As with most new things, the pluses and minuses had to be carefully tabulated to figure the overall effect.

If rainbow smelt offers a mixture of good and bad effects for the Lake ecosystem, Zebra and Quagga mussels offer a clear-cut case of negative impacts.[10] First found in Lake Michigan in 1989, they have spread like crabgrass on an August lawn. Now they cover miles of Great Lakes bottom, encrusting water intake pipes, wrecks, and every hard surface available for colonization. The damage they inflict is not simply the unsightly masses of shells upon the shoreline or the cut feet of swimmers as they unwittingly step on them. It is the damage they do to the established food chains that causes the real trouble.

Mussels feed at the bottom of the food chain. They consume phytoplankton—the microscopic plants of the water—effectively making that food unavailable to other species that would eat it: young perch, whitefish, alewives, and a host of other native fish. With fewer small fish, predators get less to eat. In the end, the top predators are affected since they indirectly depend upon the very phytoplankton the mussels removed from the bottom of the food chain. It is a long chain of cause-and-effect and not all of the effects have been taken into account by fishery biologists. In their research papers they can only offer tentative explanations, not hard-and-fast conclusions. The interactions of thousands of different species are too complicated to make sweeping generalizations.

For example, the round goby, another invader that made its appearance in 1993, eats mussels, a feature we should all applaud. But it is a rapacious feeder on fish eggs and hatchlings of a variety of native fish including sturgeon and whitefish. Is it an advantage or disadvantage? The truth is difficult to ferret out. In any case, the activities of humans will never undo the goby's effects on the lakes.

Looking at the Lake, Past, Present and Future

To an observer walking upon the beach at Clinch Park in Traverse City, the water looks clean. The sandy beach looks clean with only a few tatters of plastic marring the scene. In fact, the water is cleaner than it was eighty years ago when raw sewage entered the west arm of Grand Traverse Bay by way of the Boardman River. It is cleaner than it used to be in 1910 when the Ott sawmill efficiently got rid of mill wastes by casting them into the river.[11] Still, the water is not as it was in 1850. For one thing, a brownish slimy mass covers the rocks in shallow water. Where did that come from?

By the devious workings of ecology it comes from the presence of Zebra and Quagga mussels. They filter out particles, an action with unexpected negative consequences. In making water clear, they make bottom habitat hospitable for a green alga, *Cladophora*.[12] It grows everywhere, even tens of feet down, covering vast stretches of the floor of the Bay. In addition, freshwater biologists believe the mussels make a nutrient, phosphorus, more available to the alga. The result? Rocks covered with slime. The solution? Unknown.

Another change in the Great Lakes comes home to us every October. Situated near the Front Street bridge over the Boardman River is the fish weir, a site popular among locals and visitors in the fall. The weir blocks the passage of fish up the river. It directs them up a fish ladder to tanks where they are harvested for commercial purposes. Most of the fish are salmon: Chinook or Coho. Lake trout are taken infrequently, along with a few steelhead, a species not native to the Great Lakes. The scene at the weir provides a contrast to the Indians catching large lake trout through holes in the ice on Boardman Lake, 1859. The fishermen, their methods of capture, and the kind of fish caught are all different from that time. Over the past hundred and fifty years, the changes experienced by this great body of water and its tributaries touch every aspect of life, human and nonhuman alike.

The Boardman River, the Bay, Lake Michigan, and the Great Lakes will never return to the way they were before white settlement. The sturgeon will never populate the Great Lakes as they did before commercial fishing. Whitefish will not reach the size and numbers they attained before 1872. The lake herring will never supplant alewives and lake trout will not crowd out Pacific salmon as top predator of the Lakes. We cannot go back, but it is enough for now that we preserve a lake ecosystem that is diverse, clean, and as stable as possible. Though modest, it is a goal that does honor to those who cared for the Lakes in the past and to those who care for them now.

Logs awaiting discharge into the Boardman River (Traverse Area Historical Society)

CHAPTER 13

How We Changed the Land
*Tracing the Impacts of Settlement on
the Forests of Northern Michigan*

Before the middle of the nineteenth century the Traverse area was largely a plain of red and white pines with scattered red and white oaks mixed in. To get a feel for that forest you need to visit Interlochen State Park or the forested campus of Northwestern Michigan College. There, though they do not tower like redwoods, the trees are still quite tall, some reaching heights of a hundred feet. In the original forest, the understory was relatively open—few slender trunks cluttered the visual field at eye level.[1] Both natural and human-caused ground fire eliminated much undergrowth, exposing a dense carpet of needles and leaves which preserved moisture during the summer months, a time of year when droughts were frequent. Trailing arbutus, partridgeberry, bracken, and blueberries covered the forest floor then as it does now on the east and west sides of Boardman Lake in relict populations. Perhaps they are waiting until civilized humans move on so that they can reclaim the area once more.

Wetlands lay nearby the town: the present Kids Creek watershed was a swamp of spruce, hemlock, white cedar, and elm.[2] Where the Northern Michigan Asylum would be built in thirty-five years, water ran out of the surrounding moraines in rivulets big and small, as they do now, though in diminished amounts. Soils in the uplands are better than those near the Bay—more clay is present, for one thing. Northern Michigan hardwoods dominate the rolling hills: beech, sugar maple, eastern hemlock, red maple, and white ash. Spaces remain that preserve the ambience of that forest: the hardwoods near the former State Hospital and near Willow Hill School have never been cut.[3] Huge gray beeches grow there, most rotted out inside but still vigorous in old age. Sugar maples—some surely two hundred years old—stand straight up without a branch for forty feet, a sign that they competed for sunlight their whole lives long. They contrast with the wolf trees of the City which explode in a tangle of branches barely ten feet from the sidewalks nearby. The trees of the city grow far faster than their forest cousins.

Loggers arrived in the area even before 1850. Horace Boardman set up his sawmill at Kids Creek (then called Mill Creek) in 1847.[4] Perry Hannah bought him out and erected a steam-powered mill at the mouth of the Boardman River in 1852, expanding his operation in 1856. The great pines of the Traverse settlement were going down, though some of the oaks were spared, their wood less desirable. Still the white and red oaks stand, some of them anyway, on the west side of town and along Washington and Webster Streets. If they were human, they would remember the quiet before civilization. If human, they would feel an aching sense of loss.

Early photographs of Traverse City reveal a barren landscape. It did not take long for loggers to remove the great white and red pines and to abrade the land. Branches and brush were burned on the spot. At times fires raged so hot the very topsoil was burned off, destroying in a moment the legacy of several thousand years of organic accumulation. Mosses, lichens, and clubmosses moved in to colonize the sterile sand where the forest had grown before. The transformation from mature forest to a sandy plain, hot in summer and windswept in winter, was astounding to behold.

Yet Traverse City was spared the worst of the consuming fires of the nineteenth century: the great fires of October, 1871, which occurred all over the Great Lakes area including Chicago.[5] The summer had been dry that year and the wastes of logging and the sawdust stood thick around the villages and sawmills. A gale wind from the south sprang up ahead of an invading cold front, making primitive fire control methods useless. In Northern Michigan Manistee was hit the hardest by the ensuing blaze. This description given by an eyewitness was reprinted in the *Grand Traverse Herald,* after originally appearing in the *Grand Rapids Eagle*:

> As soon as darkness began to close in, a lurid light appeared in the southwest on the shore of Lake Michigan showing that the pine woods that line the shore were on fire. About 9 1/2 p.m. just as people were returning from evening services, the fire alarm again sounded, and everyone now was on the alert, for the wind was blowing a fierce gale. Instantly a red angry glare lighted up the western sky near the mouth of the river. The fire department rushed to the rescue. At the mouth were located the large mill and tug interests of John Canfield, with boarding house and 25 or 30 dwellings. On the beach several acres were covered with pine sawdust highly inflammable. Along the river near the piers were piled several hundred cords of dry pine slabs—fuel for tugs.
>
> Down from the circling hills on the lakeshore pounced the devouring monster. The burning sawdust whirled by the gale in fiery clouds, filled the air. Hundreds of cords of dry, pitchy slabs sent up great columns of red flame, that swayed in the air like mighty banners of fire, swept across the Manistee, two hundred feet wide, and almost instantly, like great fiery tongues licked up the government lighthouse situated one hundred and fifty feet from the north bank of the river.[6]

This account and its continuation tell us much about the fire. For one thing, sawmills were often the source of the flames. They were frequently steam-powered, the boiler fired with wood. Sparks and burning cinders escaped the stacks and blew onto ready sources of fuel: pine sawdust and the slabs cut from trees. A fierce gale, generally dry conditions: there was no stopping the fire. Traverse City was lucky. Its steam-powered mills were located on the south shore of the Bay. Sparks from the sawmill chimneys flew over the water, not the land, so the village was spared. Not so with Manistee. The *Herald* reports its losses as follows: Lost in the fire: dwellings, 157; hotels, 3; offices, 6; barns 59; saloons, 14; shops, 38; stores, 32; mills, 6. One hundred sixty-one families were made homeless by the blaze.[7] Given the fires were caused by the human abuse of the natural world, perhaps the suffering of Manistee and elsewhere was a sort of retribution for human misconduct. You do not cut down and burn a vast pine forest with impunity.

Citizens of the nineteenth century, of course, did not see it that way. Cutting the forest down and burning the slash left behind was nothing more than bringing civilization to a place that greatly needed civilizing. The inconvenience of summer fire and smoke was a price worth paying. An announcement in the *Herald* on October 12, 1871, casually remarks the air over Lake Michigan was too smoky for navigation and that several boats had laid in at Grand Haven until visibility improved. No doubt people walked about in summer dabbing their faces with wet cloths and coughing out dark mucus from their lungs. Smoke was like mosquitoes in Northern Michigan: a burden to be tolerated, not a problem that could be solved.

Logging and attendant fires destroyed the organic layer of soil in many places, took away the thick layer of pine needles and leaves which acted as a mulch to preserve soil moisture, and scalped the land, leaving it vulnerable to erosion. This created a new space for a different forest.[8] Indeed, some trees were perfectly adapted to the changed conditions. Poplar was one of them. It thrived upon open, sunny spaces. So the poplars, both trembling aspen and big-tooth, expanded throughout the north, whole villages of them joined together with underground stems, covering hills and valleys and the ancient lake bottoms that made up the land of Traverse. As they spread, the animals that lived among them came, too, especially the white-tailed deer which browsed upon the twigs and buds during much of the year. Less common before logging, they were the lucky ones, prospering as less fortunate species declined. Pine warblers, fishers, pine martins, and spruce grouse were the losers, their existence threatened by loss of old-growth swamp habitat.[9] Few people in the Northern Lower Peninsula have ever seen them in the wild.

As logging exposed the land, wetlands began to disappear. The water table began to go down as surface water ran off denuded slopes rather than sinking into the soil. The *Herald* tells of numerous artesian wells in the early Traverse settlement, ten of them in 1869.[10] Water flows out of artesian wells under pressure generated by under-

Boardman River with logs, taken before 1869. (Traverse Area Historical Society)

ground flow that proceeds from the hills surrounding the town. An impervious cap of clay prevents leakage on the way down and confines the water until it can be tapped. Artesian wells have largely disappeared from the city in recent years. One of them existed near the corner of Eighth Street and Union and another alongside the original Oleson's grocery store on East Front Street. Is their disappearance due to the diminishment of flow underground, a phenomenon possibly related to reduced absorption of rain on the hills? Perhaps. It is reasonable to suppose that human activity caused the demise of the wells.

We know from survey records that the plain surrounding Kid's Creek was once a vast wetland forest.[11] The water table was undoubtedly higher before drainage ditches were dug along highways, effectively draining the swamp. Now the area between Meijer's and West Silver Lake Road as well as low land of the Grand Traverse Commons supports invasive grasses and shrubs (particularly buckthorn) on ground that walkers tread without the discomfort of wet feet. After logging, the exposed land evaporated water faster than before, depleting soil moisture and making the area less a marsh and more a grassland. It is a story told throughout Northern Michigan and elsewhere: urbanization, habitat destruction, and the decline of wetlands. It is a story that should be told no more.

Hunting changed the land, too. Throughout the nineteenth century and into the twentieth, bear, wolves, and other predators were eliminated as they were seen as threats to humans and their farm animals. The *Grand Traverse Herald* reported bears on the Old Mission peninsula in 1859 killing pigs and farmer's dogs. In the eighteen sixties, wolves and bears were blamed for the loss of a child near Charlevoix. About the same time a posse was organized to track down and kill bears in the Williamsburg area. Though no actual attacks on humans were reported, the prevailing belief of settlers was that predators were pests and, perhaps, dangerous to people and should be hunted down whenever possible. For this reason, bears became increasingly rare and wolves disappeared altogether from the Lower Peninsula by 1910.[12] Correspondingly, animals preyed upon by wolves and bears (such as woodchucks) experienced a population increase.

If intentional activities like hunting changed land ecosystems significantly, unintentional activities such as the introduction of new species may have affected them even more. Tree diseases such as Dutch Elm Disease, introduced to this country in 1928, have changed the composition of the forest by removing keystone species. Ominously waiting in the wings are new diseases ready to wreak havoc upon the forest: Emerald Ash Borer for White Ash, Oak Wilt for Red and White Oaks, and Beech Bark Disease for the American Beech, and the Wooly Adelgid for the American Hemlock.[13] Northern Michigan never supported the American Chestnut so that Chestnut Blight, so important in the eastern United States, did not affect local forests to any great degree. Since reliable controls for recent invasive diseases have not been applied on a large scale, the forests of the future may look very different from those of today. As diseases spread, it is likely that fewer species will make up deciduous and coniferous forests of Northern Michigan. With oaks, beech, hemlock and ashes in trouble, Northern Michigan hardwoods will not resemble the forests of the past or the present. However, it is too early to predict exactly what the forest will look like even fifty years from now.

A hundred fifty years ago Morgan Bates, editor of the *Grand Traverse Herald*, visited the Pineries (the pine forest) several miles up the Boardman River. He gives his impressions in a short passage:

> In one respect we were disappointed in the appearance of the Pineries. They did not present that somber and gloomy appearance we expected. This is owing to the fact that a large proportion is Norway or Yellow Pine *[now known as Red Pine]* which grows upon an open sandy plain, with little or no underbrush. The white pine is more scattering and of much larger growth. We saw some logs three feet in diameter, all "clear." These Pineries are six miles wide north and south, and extend about fifteen miles to the eastward, on either bank of the Boardman River, which runs through the centre of the tract. The banks of the river are high and steep, affording great facilities for getting the logs into the water. The current is strong and the water as clear as crystal, with a white gravelly bottom.[14]

As we read, we cannot help but feel a sense of loss. If only we could experience such a place… If only a hundred acres were saved out of the thousands that were destroyed… If only the trees were seen not only as a commodity but as a benediction to us all… If only the Pineries would come back as they used to be after a hundred or even two hundred years… But such wishful thinking bears no fruit. We can only care for the land that has been passed along to us. We can do no more. But is not that a task worthy of our energy and our heart's work?

The railroad bridge across the Boardman River, before 1883.

CHAPTER 14

Life at the End of a Peninsula
How Geography Shapes our Community

People who live towards the end of a peninsula are unique. They do not entertain visitors on the way to other destinations. Great highways do not extend through their domain. Far removed from centers of population, they do not attract large industries since transportation costs would be excessive to locate manufacturing plants in such a place.

To invite residents and visitors, the end of a peninsula must provide attractions to overcome the natural deficits: jobs supplied by entrepreneurs, a physical resource such as a seemingly inexhaustible source of pine lumber, or beautiful scenery that beckons visitors to stay. Isolation is overcome only through much effort. That is the way it has always been in Northern Michigan and it is the way it is now.

The isolation of the Grand Traverse area from the rest of Michigan and the United States generally is a historical fact. When hundreds of covered wagons headed west over the Oregon Trail in the year 1854, young Perry Hannah was walking on snowshoes from Traverse City to Grand Rapids, an arduous six day trek. His account of the journey tells us much about the tribulations of travel in those days.

> I made my first trip to the "outside world" on snowshoes. Soon after the first of January,1854, I left Traverse City when there was hardly a single house outside the limits of the city to Grand Rapids. The snow was plump three feet deep, light as feathers and not a single step could be taken without Indian snowshoes. I furnished myself with two Indian packers for carrying supplies. It took six days to make the trip from here to Grand Rapids. The first settlement we reached was Big Rapids, some five or six miles this side of the forks of the Muskegon River.
>
> The wolves got on our track before the first night's camping. They were not troublesome in the least until we had made our camp fires in the evening; then a tremendous howling was set up and continued during the whole night. We were not in the least troubled as to their contact with us, but they broke up our sleep. As soon as we left our camp in the morning, they followed us and picked up any scraps that might be left. They continued with us till we were out of the woods.
>
> There was not a single sign of a trail of any kind to travel by which compelled us to use our compass, as very little sunshine can be seen at that season of the year beneath the thick timber that then shrouded the whole country. That was the most tedious journey I ever experienced in the early days of Grand Traverse.

Hannah underlines the isolation of Traverse City as he tells of this exchange he had with state legislators in the winter of 1857:

> When the legislature adjourned, early in the spring, some of the members came and shook hands with me and said, "I suppose you have to go on to your home all the way by stage." This was very amusing to me, coming from state legislators, when I knew my trip had to be made 'afoot and alone' through the long woods.

It was not until 1869 that the Northport-Newaygo road was completed, connecting the Grand Traverse region with downstate cities.

The expansion of the telegraph, which often paralleled the extension of railroads and highways, only reached Traverse City in 1871, long after lines had joined Grand Rapids, Kalamazoo, Lansing and other cities to the economic centers of the nation. Hired Indian mail carriers were the only link to the outside world in these early years. The weekly local newspaper, the *Grand Traverse Herald*, could not give a full report on Lincoln's death because initial written accounts were unclear, requiring readers to wait another week to learn the details of the assassination. Meanwhile, downstate cities enjoyed regular news reports from Washington and elsewhere.

It might be supposed that waterways could supply a ready avenue of transportation to Northern Michigan. After all, from Indian canoes and French voyageurs to the steamships of the nineteenth century the Great Lakes have provided a highway for the movement of goods and people. Shipping was not without its problems, however. Compared to railroads, it was slow, sometimes dangerous—especially in the gales of autumn—and was impossible during the ice-bound months of the year beginning in December and sometimes extending into April. D.C Leach in his *History of the Grand Traverse Region* writes of the trepidation with which sea captains regarded Grand Traverse Bay, seeing it as a body of water riddled with shoals and boulders. It was easier for all to bypass the Bay and proceed to Wisconsin and Illinois, thereby transporting settlers further west. Unable to resist paying homage to his home town, the newspaperman quotes a fabled captain of a Great Lakes boat:

> Captain Blake, once well known on the lakes, is said to have been the only one of his time who knew the Grand Traverse country, and was disposed to do it justice. He frequently told his passengers, when off the bay, on the way to their more distant homes to the west, that they were passing the most beautiful country ever beheld.

When the transcontinental railroad was completed in 1869, the Traverse area was as yet unconnected to the railroad system. It would be three more years before the first line reached Traverse City. Leach describes in detail the frustration of Northern Michigan legislators at the failure of the railroad companies to make good on their promises of extending lines to the north. Finally, after much jousting in Lansing, they achieved their goal: the Grand Rapids and Indiana Company began construction on a line that opened the north to settlement. It almost missed Traverse City, though. Only through gathering private subscriptions did Perry Hannah and others raise enough money to extend the rails to the city in 1872. Without that effort, Elk Rapids (or some other village) would have become the largest city in Northern Michigan.

The impact of the railroad cannot be overstated. Leach tells of the changes:

> As the road pushed northward, settlers flocked in, dotting the wilderness in advance of it with their log cabins clustering around, and giving new life to the little villages already in existence, and founding new ones along the line of the road, even in advance of its completion. The good time long waited for had come, and the injustice of the past was nearly forgotten in the prosperity of the present.

Settlers come only with an expectation of creating decent lives for themselves. Northern Michigan had received negative press through newspaper writing of Horace Greely in 1859. According to Leach, Greely wrote that the northern half of the Lower Peninsula was cold and uninviting to the cultivator, diversified by vast swamps, sterile, gravelly knolls, and dense forests of but moderately valuable timber not yet readily accessible, so that its settlement was likely to be slow, and its population sparse for generations. After such a review, local boosters realized that a promotional campaign would have to be undertaken. The virtues of Northern Michigan would have to be displayed for all to see.

And they were. Morgan Bates, first editor of the *Grand Traverse Herald*, described the area in gracious prose, its beauty and its prospects for development, as well as a too avid insistence that the climate was not too severe:

> The scenery around the entire Bay is delightful, and the climate as healthy and agreeable as can be found in any part of North America. The leading timber is hard maple, interspersed with beech, ash, oak, basswood, pine, cedar, hemlock, and other varieties; and the soil is as rich and productive as that of Western New York. We have no early frosts to injure the

> crops. The first heavy frost at Traverse City this season occurred on the night of the 25th of October, since our arrival here. Some very light frosts were experienced as early as the first of that month, but none previous to that time.

His stories found their way east to be read by readers charmed by his accounts of Indians, the great pineries of Michigan, fish of unbelievable size, and farmland that could be bought inexpensively. Indeed, they likely attracted a few hardy souls ready to take on the physical hardships, the isolation, and the voracious summer mosquitoes. In 1873 a fine portrait of Traverse City (See page 1) was created by the town fathers, a lithograph which displayed the virtues of this place: good fishing and hunting, farming, logging, possibilities for commerce of all kinds. Like many small communities struggling to survive and prosper, the city knew the importance of advertising.

At the end of a long peninsula prosperity and a burgeoning population are far from certain. However, writing in the *Herald* in 1869, Leach was prescient as he listed the reasons Traverse City would overcome the barriers associated with its location. First, he observed the city was already a commercial center and later development would funnel naturally towards it. Second, the coming railroad would enrich the region. Third, logging would bring in wealth. Fourth, he predicted the success of fruit farming in the area, a remarkable guess at a time before cherries, apples, peaches, and plums had been widely planted. Fifth, he told of local entrepreneurs who had already made a mark in the world. Sixth, he foresaw the growth of the tourist industry even before comfortable resorts had been established locally. Seventh, he saw the development of cultural amenities—churches and schools and "whatever is calculated to promote the public good" as a means to attract and retain residents. Certainly Interlochen Arts Academy, Northwestern Michigan College, and local hospitals have fulfilled this vision. One hundred forty years after Leach's essay, we can appreciate his understanding of the Traverse region and its future residents. In modern parlance, he nailed it.

Still, development did not come easily. Settlers and late arrivals had to give something up to live here: warmer winters, fertile soil of farms further south, higher wages in fledgling industries, time-consuming trips to the centers of business and culture. It hasn't changed since Leach's time—so why do we stay? I would argue it is the power of land and water.

Traditionally, people have always hunted and fished in Northern Michigan, but the attachment to Nature goes beyond these sports. The woods and waters are simply enjoyed. Reports of ice conditions on the Bay make headlines in the local paper. Accounts of abundant snowfall generate angst as well as good-humored appreciation. Sightings of snowy owls and peregrine falcons draw the curious to locations within the city limits. Those persons that fill wetlands and pollute the water are not received favorably, even if they claim to be creating jobs. People here care about the environment. They would not trade what they have for a large manufacturing plant that would destroy their way of life, even if it would improve their financial well-being. That is the attraction of the area, the magnetism which overcomes the handicap of its place at the end of a long peninsula. We love where we live.

Augusta Louise Rosenthal-Thompson, picture taken about 1906.

CHAPTER 15

Say, Sis, Is the Doctor In?
The Life of Augusta Rosenthal-Thompson, M.D.

INTRODUCTION

Augusta Louise Rosenthal-Thompson was a courageous woman and a gifted physician. She undertook the study of medicine when enrolling in medical school was an act of courage for any woman. She chose to practice medicine in a primitive community lacking many of the amenities of civilization. Recognizing the shortcomings of her education, she pursued the study of medicine in Europe, thereby putting her personal life at risk. Upon her return to Traverse City, she brought back new medical techniques she learned abroad, published research papers in medical journals, and continued her medical practice, treating her patients with kindness and warmth, thereby helping them to deal with the suffering that attends human life. In writing this short biography, it brings me special joy to honor the achievements of this remarkable person.

The Life of Augusta Rosenthal-Thompson

In 1886 the Traverse settlement was a raw and dirty place. Front Street was unpaved and rutted, troubled with blowing dust or sticky mud in the summer months and covered with snow and ice during the long winter. The Bay pounded then as now whenever the wind blew from the North, though the drum and crash of the waves was often drowned out by the blast of locomotive and boat whistles at the busy dock area. Trees were few, the great pines having been logged off twenty years before, though the scarred landscape supported a few oaks, their hardwood having protected them from the rapacious saws of Hannah-Lay Company loggers.

Houses were modest in 1886, and most businesses occupied frame buildings on Front and Union Streets with one grand exception: the Hannah-Lay Mercantile Building at the corner of Union and Front. Three stories high and a half a block long, it was the finest store north of Grand Rapids. Somehow the townspeople felt it pointed to a bright future for this isolated place so distant from the roads that carried men to the fabled riches of the west. Meanwhile, it stood as a curious pyramid in a desert, visitors wondering if it was out of place in the dust and mud and snow dirtied by human traffic.

So, too, did the Northern Michigan Asylum surprise people with its unexpected elegance. Its imposing yellow brick walls, cupolas and gates were things of a European castle transplanted to this unlikely place of Northern Michigan. Constructed only one year before, it still inspired awe in the loggers, mill workers, and farmers that visited the town only occasionally. Of course, what went on inside its walls was something they did not want to think about.

Wooden bridges crossed the Boardman River north and south on Union Street. As they still do, people would stand upon them to fish or to stare at the flowing water which carried a load of logs, sawdust, and rubbish, the accompaniments of white settlement that had begun forty years earlier, to the cleaner waters of West Bay only a mile away. A flour mill stood at the Union Street dam, its presence creating wagon traffic along thoroughfares not adorned with trees and lawns. The clatter of wheels, the snorts of the horses and the shouts of the drivers had replaced the cries of towhees, warblers, and song sparrows within the memories of middle-aged men. The wilderness had left this place, but it lingered still in places not too far away.

This was the place to which a young woman arrived in the spring of the year just after the melt of the ice on the Bay. Her appearance was striking: dark hair composed in curls at the front and tied back in the style of the day, high forehead and angular features, with large, dark eyes that surveyed people and things with startling penetration. She carried herself as women of that day would, with proper carriage, head held erect, shoulders back, striding rapidly forward at a faster pace than custom dictated for women of the time. Slender and tall, she commanded the attention of passers-by, not simply because she was an unaccompanied woman in this plain village, but because she grasped a small black bag in her hand, a sure sign that she practiced medicine. She was a doctor.

In the last part of the nineteenth century, women doctors were not unheard-of, but they were uncommon. By 1900, one in five physicians was a woman, a proportion that would not change throughout the first half of the twentieth century. In Michigan relatively more women may have been trained since the University of Michigan had been among the first of the nation's medical schools to admit women, the first female students entering the Medical School in 1870. The brave figure that arrived in Traverse, medical bag in hand, was Augusta Louise Rosenthal, an 1884 graduate of University of Michigan Medical School. At age 25, she elected to serve this backwards community in Northern Michigan for reasons that are not entirely clear to us. Perhaps it was the challenge of it all.

Dr. Rosenthal's University of Michigan Medical School graduation picture.

A challenge it was. In her first advertisement in the local paper, the *Grand Traverse Herald*, she announces her occupation: "Physician and Surgeon" followed by "Diseases of Women and Children a Specialty," and then, bravely, "Country Calls Promptly Answered." In the early years of her practice her "country calls" were carried out by means of horseback, carriage, snowshoes, even ice-boat and railroad handcar. On one occasion she even had to share space with beer kegs in the back of a brewery wagon. Whenever she ventured out to visit her patients, she had to keep an eye out for a lanterns lit in the windows of country homes. That signal would indicate that a family had need for the doctor.

Beyond the inconveniences of such travel—the cold, the heat, the bloodsucking insects—she sometimes had to face real dangers in this primitive place. One winter she was called to attend a patient that required a journey across the frozen Lake. As the Doctor and her driver went out on the ice, cracks began to open up and the team was forced to jump them. To make matters worse, the driver had his foot trampled by the horses and was unable to help. Dr. Rosenthal took the reins in hand and somehow guided them across the failing ice to safety. Summer brought its dangers, too: fire. At the edge of a forest fire, her horse shying from the flames, she put a blanket over its head and led it through the smoke, successfully arriving at her patient's home. Later in old age, she wondered if her poor eyesight did not result from the irritation of the smoke and heat.

At this time medicine was practiced largely in the homes of patients. Understandably, it was impossible to bring all of the medical equipment required for treatment. Once the Doctor was forced to tear up her own petticoat to provide packing for a wound. Another time, in the absence of a catheter, she improvised an empty vial of codeine to relieve urinary retention in a child. In setting broken bones and performing amputations no doubt she converted many kitchens into operating rooms. This was medicine practiced in its most elemental form far from clinic and hospital. Before the days of health insurance and office help, the doctor's fees for her varied services were on a sliding scale ranging from a half dozen donuts to one thousand dollars.

With all of this medical drama, it is easy to forget that Augusta Louise Rosenthal was a young, unmarried woman when she began her practice in Traverse City. Her youthful appearance explains her first patient inquiring upon mounting the steps to her office on Front Street, "Say, Sis, is the Doctor in?" Not surprisingly, she soon met a young doctor, Isaac A. Thompson, and they fell in love, marrying in 1887. According to a later newspaper account, Dr. Thompson had "a personality that was attractive and was of an exceptionally generous disposition, many times going out of his way to give aid and relief to others in distress," praise that was freely given to many in the press at the time, but probably containing a kernel of truth nevertheless. In 1895 he would run against Perry Hannah for mayor. He lost, as might be expected, going up against the founder of the City, but the campaign demonstrates the degree of his popularity. Partitioning their practice, the two doctors complemented each other, she concentrating on the diseases of children and women, and he upon those of men. It seemed at the outset an ideal match both professionally and personally.

Their first child, Isaac Alonzo, Jr. (called Jackie by his parents) was born in 1889. Tragically, he died in childhood of diphtheria in 1896. Though he received the best treatment medicine could offer—even getting an injection of the newly discovered diphtheria antitoxin—he weakened, contracted pneumonia, and passed away, saying in the remembered words of his mother, "Tomorrow I will be with my best friend, Jesus." "He was," the Doctor added as she recalled the evening of his death years later. That same evening she attended another child stricken with the same disease. He, too, died.

She was devastated. Her medical training was inadequate and her own child—and how many others—had succumbed as a result. She would leave Traverse City and learn more: she would visit hospitals in New York City, London, Berlin, and Vienna. Her ignorance of medicine would not be a reason children would die from diseases like pneumonia or diphtheria. She would leave this place with its beautiful Bay and learn how to treat gravely ill children.

Living in a society vastly different from that of the late nineteenth century, we may not understand the significance of a married woman's decision to leave her husband and community for two years. At that time, wives stayed with their husbands, no matter what. If they did not, they could be accused of desertion, an offense that could be grounds for a divorce. Even though her marriage might be endangered by her resolve to learn more medicine abroad, she would not change her mind. She left within months of Jackie's death.

Her journey began at the New York Polyclinic. Following a six month stay there, she continued her post-graduate work in Europe, visiting hospitals in many countries.

At that time, German medicine was far ahead of American. Her new training would be thoroughly up-to-date, cutting edge with regard to new treatments for childhood diseases. With her mother and father both of German extraction, she was a capable speaker of German. In Germany or another European country, she learned about blood transfusion, a technique she would bring back to Traverse City. Over the course of her stay she attended four courses with senior students at the University of Vienna, including pediatrics with famed Professor von Weiderhof, personal physician of Emperor Fran Joseph of Austria. His recommendation enabled her to study in Berlin over the objections of those who felt it was inappropriate for a woman to engage in medicine. Prejudice knows no national boundaries.

Dr. Rosenthal-Thompson was an adventurous traveler. Observing a funeral procession in Germany, she inquired who had died. Told it was Johannes Brahms, the famous composer, she resolved to attend the funeral even though women did not ordinarily go to such ceremonies. Directions given her by a bystander enabled her to find the open grave near shrubbery and to listen to the funeral proceedings without being seen. She was the only woman in attendance.

Upon her return to Traverse City, she was met at the railroad station by the parents of a playmate of her son Jackie who had died two years before. Their son was ill with diphtheria and was in grave condition: Could the doctor help? With her knowledge enhanced by her trip abroad, she was able to save the boy. Her voyage to learn more about the diseases of childhood had not been in vain!

Here began a darker period in the Doctor's life. Her marriage to Isaac Thompson crumbled. As predicted, she was accused of desertion by her husband and the Court found that to be a just basis for ending the marriage, granting the divorce in 1902. Isaac Thompson married soon after and moved his medical practice to Grand Rapids. At this time Rosenthal-Thompson moved regularly, spending time in the Park Place in 1900, establishing a residence at 519 State Street for several years with a brother and sister, listing her residence the same as her office location in the Traverse City State Bank building in 1907-08, and giving 716 Washington as her address in 1909-10 Polk Directory. Clearly this was a difficult time in her life.

Isaac A. Thompson died unexpectedly in 1909, his obituary meriting front page prominence in the *Evening Record*, continuing on a second page. It detailed his early life in Traverse City as a physician, his commitment to the Elks and Masonic fraternities as well as the Knights Templars, his marriage to Alma Dupres and the births of his two sons in 1905 and 1907. Surprisingly, it did not mention his earlier marriage, nor the son that died in 1896. At this time, perhaps because of social custom, little was said of the dissolution of the marriage and subsequent remarriage of the husband. Some things are best left unspoken.

Whatever the distress of a broken relationship, there was always medicine to practice. In 1905 she read a meticulously researched paper before the Michigan State Medical Society meeting at Petoskey, Michigan, concerning rectal examination of children. She gave presentations before the Traverse City Women's Club concerning healthy living. She participated in the Grand Traverse Physicians' Association and was a founding member of the Michigan branch of the Women's Academy of Medicine. Still, the practice of medicine was not the same as in those raw days when she had first arrived in the City. In these days before the First World War things were quieter—one of the largest employers, the Oval Wood Dish Company, had left town and the city had entered a malaise. She decided to move to Grand Rapids.

So she did. There she began a practice, but soon discontinued it to move to Philadelphia to treat the wives and children of World War I veterans at no charge. One wonders if she regarded this venture as a way to prove her patriotism, this woman of German background who could speak German so well. Whatever the reasons, she spent time serving in a dispensary in Philadelphia, helping the war effort in a manner appropriate to her role as a physician who specialized in treating illnesses of women and children. After the war she returned to Grand Rapids to resume her practice.

Over the course of her practice in Grand Rapids throughout the twenties, she would remember this period as an easy time with hospitals, ambulances, and good roads at her service. She practiced medicine in the style of those days, with home visits and office consultations. Her warm personality broke down barriers between the doctor and her patients. ""Though I intended to specialize in pediatrics, I soon found that when

Dr. Rosenthal-Thompson's residence on State Street.

I had a child to care for I also had the rest of the family as patients—and friends." For her, medicine was not simply diagnosis and treatment, but was a means of participating in the lives of others, helping them however she could.

About 1930, the Doctor retired from her practice. She purchased a house in Berrien Springs, Michigan, and commenced a long retirement. Living with her brother Theodore and a sister, Florence Lockhart, she spent her days both keeping abreast of the events of the day and remembering the early days spent in Traverse City. A full-page newspaper article in the *Grand Rapids Herald* brought her story before the public in 1947. Two years later a story appeared in the *Medical Woman's Journal* with her remembrances of the past. In 1954, at the age of 94, she died in Berrien Springs. She elected to be buried in Oakwood Cemetery in Traverse City, the place in which she had begun her medical practice so long ago.

There she lies in a broad open space near a large oak tree. The sexton of the cemetery tells us that there is no headstone and that she was buried beside the grave of little Jackie, who died so long ago of the diphtheria she could not cure. Jackie, too, lies without a marker, the two of them together at last. Though her grave is unmarked, her achievements live on in the patients she helped even to the present day.

Timeline of Events in the Life of Augusta Louise Rosenthal-Thompson

June 1, 1859: Born in Fort Wayne, Indiana, the third of eleven children.

1876: Her mother dies of cancer. Augusta Louise acts as mother to the children.

1884: Graduates from the University of Michigan School of Medicine.

1886: Begins her practice in village of Traverse City, Michigan.

1887: Married Isaac A. Thompson.

1889: Her son, Isaac Jack Alonzo Thompson Jr., is born.

1896: Her son Isaac dies.

1896-97: Leaves Traverse City for extended post-graduate study.

1899-1900: Resumes practice in Traverse City.

1902: Is divorced from Isaac A. Thompson.

1911-12: Moves to Grand Rapids, Michigan, to begin medical practice.

1917-18: Serves as doctor to women and children of war veterans of WWI.

1918: Resumes medical practice in Grand Rapids.

1930: Retires from medical practice.

March 21, 1954: Dies in Spring Lake, Ottawa County, Michigan.

Sources

CHAPTER 1 • The First Portrait of Traverse City

1. All of the maps mentioned in this article were obtained from the Traverse Area Historical Society, 322 Sixth Street, Traverse City, Michigan. Some may be viewed on-line at TraverseHistory.org.

2. Brief biographies of these early settlers may be found in Wilson, Robert E., *Grand Traverse Legends, Vol.1 The Early Years 1838-1860*. (Grand Traverse Pioneer and Historical Society, 322 Sixth St., Traverse City, MI 49684.)

3. A general outline of events important to Traverse City (such as the building of the railroad) can be obtained from Wakefield, Lawrence, *Queen City of the North: An Illustrated History of Traverse City From Its Beginnings to the 1980's*. (Traverse City, MI: Village Press Inc. 1988.)

4. "William Holdsworth Dead," *Evening Record*, 9 Sept. 1907, 1.

CHAPTER 2 • Listening to Dissonant Voices

"Flint Leading the State," *Record-Eagle*, 24 Apr 1917: 1.

"Incurs Wrath of Mob When He Fails to Rise For National Anthem," *Traverse City Record-Eagle*, 13 Jun, 1917: 1,3.

"Karl Temple Arrested," *Record-Eagle*, 4 Feb. 1918: 1. Also, 9 Feb 1918, 1.

Meltzer, Milton, *Ain't Gonna Study War No More*, Harper and Rowe, NY, 1985.

"Memorial Day Is Here Again!", *Honest Opinion*, 29 May 1919: 1.

"Mrs. Perry Takes a Whack At Industrial and Social Conditions," *Traverse City Press*, 23 Feb. 1917: 1.

"Ten-Year-Olds Are Patriotic," *Record-Eagle*, 26 May 1917: 1.

"Unity the Country's Need in War," *Record-Eagle*, editorial, 3 Apr 1917: 4.

"We Must Obey the Leader's Orders," *Record-Eagle*, editorial, 27 Apr 1917: 4.

Zinn, Howard, *A People's History of the United States 1492–present*. New York: Harper Perennial Modern Classics, 2003.

CHAPTER 3 • Celebrating the Fourth in Northwestern Michigan

Applebaum, Diana Karter, *The Glorious Fourth, An American Holiday, An American History*, NY: Facts on File, 1989.

"Boats Had Big Crowd," *Evening Record*, July 5, 1906. 1.

"Celebrated the Fourth," (Traverse City) *Evening Record*, July 5, 1906, 1.

"Celebration Notes "(account by Thomas T. Bates, editor), *Morning Record*, July 5, 1899, 2+.

"Expecting Huge Crowd on the Fourth," *Traverse City Record-Eagle*, July 3, 1946, 1.

"Glorious Fourth," editorial, *Record-Eagle*, July 3, 1914, 3.

"Grand Festival of Fun" advertisement, *Grand Traverse Herald*, "June 22, 1899, 3.

"A Grand Pageant," (Traverse City) *Morning Record*, July 1, 1899, 1.

"Local News," *Grand Traverse Herald*, July 4, 1876. 3.

Rauber, William J., "The Flying Allens: Aeronauts, Innovators," (Family reminiscences about early ballooning), www.balloonlife.com/webarch/allensmoke.htm.

"Today We Celebrate,"*Morning Record*, July 4, 1899, 1.

"Twelve Thousand Gather Here For the General Observance of a Patriotically Sane Fourth," *Traverse City Record-Eagle*, July 5, 1918, 1+.

Warren, Louis S., *Buffalo Bill's America: William Cody and the Wild West Show*, NY: Alfred A. Knopf, 2005.

CHAPTER 4 • From Doctor's Visits to the Modern Hospital

Barnard, H.E. *35th Annual Report of the Indiana State Board of Health For the Fiscal and Board Year Ending Sept. 30, 1916 and For the Statistical Year Ending Dec. 31, 1916*, Fort Wayne, IN: Fort Wayne Printing Co., 197.

Crellin, John K., *A Social History of Medicines in the Twentieth Century*, Philadelphia: Hawthorne Press, 2004.

Flexner, Abraham, *Medical Education in the United States and Canada: A Report to the Carnegie Foundation for the Advancement of Teaching*, Bulletin 4, 1910.

"Grand Traverse Hospital Report for the Year 1909," *Evening Record*, 26 Jan. 1910, 3.

Leavitt, Judith Walzer, "A Worrying Profession: The Domestic Environment of Medical Practice in Mid-19th Century America" in *Sickness and Health in America*, 130.

Numbers, Ronald and Warner, Harley, "The Maturation of American Medical Science" in Leavitt, Judith Walzer and Numbers, Ronald L., *Sickness and Health in America: Readings in the History of Medicine and Public Health*, University of Wisconsin Press, Madison, WI, 1997, 87.

Starr, Paul, *The Social Transformation of American Medicine*, New York: Basic Books, 1982.

Chapter 5 • Of Vagrants, Poor Funds, and Poor Houses

City of Traverse City, Official Proceedings of the City Commission, 1901, 1904, obtained at the City Clerk's Office, Governmental Center, Boardman St., Traverse City, MI.

County Infirmary (Poorhouse) Residents from the 1910 United States Federal Census, www.poorhousestory.com/MI_Allegan_1910Census.htm.

Golden, Olivia A. *Assessing the New Federalism: Eight Years Later.* New Urban Institute, Washington, D.C. 2005.

Hadock, Olave, "Hospital's Doors Closed, But Memories Linger." *Preview.* July 26, 1982, Reference Department, Traverse City Public Library.

Hunter, Robert, *Poverty*, NY: MacMillan Co., 1904.

Michigan Department of State, Annual Abstract of the Reports of the Superintendents of the Poor, 1876-1903.

Patterson, James, *America's Struggle Against Poverty in the Twentieth Century.* Cambridge, MA.: Harvard University Press, 2000.

Pimpore, Stephen, *The New Victorians: Poverty, Politics, and Propaganda in the Gilded Ages.* NY: The New Press, 2004.

Polk's Traverse City and Grand Traverse County Directory: For the Year Ending Nov. 1st, 1904, Detroit: R.L. Polk & Co., 1904.

Chapter 6 • The Veterans Memorial Highway

"Announces Inscriptions And Placing of Memorial Tablets," *Record-Eagle*, March 27, 1924, 1, 8.

"Federation Asks Advice As To Placing County Hero Memorial," *Record-Eagle*, March 14, 1924, 1.

"Tablets to be in the Program Memorial Day," *Record-Eagle*, May 27, 1924, 1+.

"Maples to be Planted as Memorials," *Record-Eagle*, May 3, 1923, 1.

"Memorial Tree Will Be Placed for Each Hero," *Traverse City Record-Eagle*, April 25, 1923, 1+.

"Paid in Full," *Record-Eagle*, July 1, 1924.

Chapter 7 • Crime and Justice A Century Ago

Browning, Frank, and Gerass, John, *The American Way of Crime*, New York: G.P. Putnam's Sons, 1980.

Friedman, Lawrence M., *Crime and Punishment in American History*, New York: Basic Books, 1993.

The Grand Traverse County Jail Record, Michigan State Archives, 71-103, Box 5 of 6, Lansing, MI.

McDonald, Arthur, *Abnormal Man: being essays on Education and Crime and Related Subjects with Digests of Literature and a Bibliography*, Gov. Printing Office, Washington, D.C., 1893.

Official Proceedings of the City Commission, 1902-03, Report of the Police Department to the City, April 1, 1902-April 1, 1903, submitted by John Rennie, Chief of Police. Office of the City Clerk, Traverse City, MI, 400 Boardman Ave., Traverse City, MI 49685.

Record of Ordinances: City of Traverse City, 1895-Dec. 2, 1918, Office of the City Clerk, Traverse City, MI, 400 Boardman Ave., Traverse City, MI 49685.

Thiel, Homer, *The Grand Traverse County Jail Book: 1870-1906*, published by Members of the French-Canadian Society of Michigan for the Grand Traverse County Region. Copy obtainable at the Traverse Area Public Library, Traverse City, MI.

Chapter 8 • Where's the Park on Park Street?

Fidler, Richard. *Glimpses of Grand Traverse Past: Reflections on a Local History.* Traverse City, MI: Grand Traverse Pioneer and Historical Society, 322 Sixth Street, Traverse City, MI, 49684, 2008.

General Land Office Notes. Record group 89-74. Natural Resources 8/14/4-8, Vol. 14, State Archives of Michigan, Lansing.

An Honor and an Ornament: Public School Buildings in Michigan. State Historic Preservation Office, Michigan Historical Center, Michigan Department of History, Arts, and Libraries, Sept. 2003. www.michiganhistory.org

Wilson, Robert, *Grand Traverse Legends, Vol. 1: The Early Years 1838-1860.* Grand Traverse Pioneer and Historical Society, 322 Sixth St, Traverse City, MI 49684, 2004.

Sources for Chapter 9 • Of Obedience, Truthfulness, and Self-Control and Chapter 10 • Many Wonderful Transitions

Grob, Gerald, *Mental Illness and American Society 1870-1940*, Princeton, NJ: Princeton University Press, 1983.

Money, John, *The Destroying Angel: Sex, Fitness, and Food in the Legacy of Degeneracy Theory*, Buffalo, NY: Prometheus Books, 1985.

Oosterhuis, Harry, *Stepchildren of Nature: Krafft-Ebing, Psychiatry, and the Making of Sexual Identity*, Chicago: University of Chicago Press, 2000.

Proceedings of the Sanitary Convention held at Traverse City, August 24 and 25, 1887. Supplement to the Report of the Michigan State Board of Health for the Year 1887. Item no. PM600-030806 Traverse Area Historical Society, 322 Sixth St., Traverse City, MI, 49684.

Report of the Board of Trustees of the Northern Michigan Asylum at Traverse City, June 30, 1910. Lansing: Wynkoop Hallenbeck Crawford Printers, 1910. Obtainable at the Traverse Area District Library, Traverse City, MI

Shorter, Edward, *A History of Psychiatry*, New York: John Wiley and Sons, 1997.

Chapter 11 • What Do Old Textbooks Tell Us of the Past?

Dodge, Richard Elwood, *Dodge's Advanced Geography*, New York: Rand McNally & Company, 1904.

Gould, Stephen Jay, *The Mismeasure of Man*, New York: W.W. Norton Company, 1981, 1996.

Hunter, George W., *A Civic Biology*, New York: American Book Company, 1914.

Mondale, Sarah and Patton, Sarah B. (ed.s), *School: The Story of American Public Education*, Boston: Beacon Press, 2001.

Morris, Charles, *Pictorial History of the United States*, Philadelphia: John C. Winston Company, 1901.

Nietz, John A., *Old Textbooks*, Pittsburg: University of Pittsburg Press, 1961.

Pieper, Charles J., Beauchamp, Wilbur L., Orlin, Frank D., *Everyday Problems in Biology*, New York: Scott, Foresman and Company, 1931.

Chapter 12 • How We Changed the Lake

1. "Boardman Lake," *Grand Traverse Herald*, 18 Feb. 1859, 4.

2. Descriptions of fish taken in the Lakes in early historical times can be found in Bogue, Margaret Beattie, *Fishing the Great Lakes: An Environmental History, 1783-1933*, (Madison: University of Wisconsin Press, 2000.)

3. Descriptions of the heyday and decline of sturgeon can be found in Dave Dempsey's books, *Ruin and Recovery: Michigan's Rise as a Conservation Leader*, (Ann Arbor: University of Michigan Press, 2001) and *On the Brink: The Great Lakes in the 21st Century*, (East Lansing: Michigan State University Press, 2004.)

4. Notices of sturgeon taken from the Boardman and the Platt Rivers are dated June 3, 1869 and June 10, 1869 in the *Grand Traverse Herald*.

5. Bogue, previously cited, tells of the decline of whitefish, 150-153.

6. A classic among students of Great Lakes fish, Hubbs, Carl L. and Lagler, Karl F. *Fishes of the Great Lakes Region*, (Ann Arbor: University of Michigan Press, 1947) describes native and introduced fish species, giving ranges of the grayling as well other interesting historical information.

7. *Ruin and Recovery*, 23-24 tells the story of the extinction of the grayling in Michigan.

8. Emery, Lee, *Review of Fish Species Introduced Into the Great Lakes*, 1819-1974, (Technical Report No. 45, Great Lakes Fishery Commission, April 1985) summarizes fish introductions into the Great Lakes before 1974.

9. Records of fish caught by biologists in the Great Lakes area can be viewed at UMMZ Fish Collection Search http://141.211.243.52/ummzlong/index.php?table_name=ummz This database has items dating from the nineteenth century. The collection extends to the twenty-first century.

10. Information about recent introductions of organisms into Lake Michigan is given in Clapp, David F. and Horns, William, [Eds]. *The State of Lake Michigan in 2005*. (Great Lakes Fish Comm. Spec. Pub. 08-02.)

11. The history behind the clean-up of the Boardman River is given in Fidler, Richard, *Glimpses of Grand Traverse Past:Reflections on a Local History*, Grand Traverse Pioneer and Historical Society, Traverse City, MI, 2008.

12. Information about *Cladophora* was obtained at the Great Lakes Water Institute website, University of Wisconsin, http://www.glwi.uwm.edu/research/aquaticecology/cladophora/ Harvey Bootsma and John Janssen are the authors of the article, *Cladophora*.

CHAPTER 13 • How We Changed the Land

1. For descriptions of pre-settlement forests, see Donald L. Dickmann, and Larry A. Leefers, *The Forests of Michigan*, Ann Arbor, (University of Michigan Press, 2003), chap. 5.

2. Surveyors' records indicate tree composition. The relevant record for Kids Creek is General Land Office Notes. Record group 89-74. Natural Resources 6/14/4-8, Vol.14, State Archives of Michigan, Lansing.

3. Perry Hannah claimed virgin hardwoods occupied the hills above the proposed Northern Michigan Asylum in 1884 as he made his case in front of the state legislature in that year.

4. The earliest history of Boardman and Perry Hannah in Traverse City is given in Robert E. Wilson, *Grand Traverse Legends, Vol. I, The Early Years 1838-1860*. (Grand Traverse Pioneer and Historical Society, 322 Sixth St. Traverse City, MI 49684, 2004).

5. Dickmann and Leefers tells of the October, 1871 fires on pp.152-158.

6. "The Manistee Fire," *Grand Traverse Herald*, 6 Oct. 1871, Supplement, 2.

7. "The Manistee Fire," *Herald*, 16 Nov. 1871, 4.

8. Dickmann and Leefers, p. 169.

9. A table showing animals associated with early successional forests and late successional forests (old growth) is given in Dickmann and Leefers, p. 206.

10. "Artesian wells," *Grand Traverse Herald*, 25 Jul. 1895, 5.

11. See note three.

12. The Michigan Department of Natural Resources gives a history of wolves in Michigan at http://www.michigan.gov/dnr/0,1607,7-153-10370_12145_12205-32569--,00.html#Michigan%20History

13. A summary of tree diseases is presented at many websites. A notable site is http://forestry.about.com/od/diseases/tp/An-Index-of-Common-Tree-Diseas.htm

14. Morgan tells about his day in the "Pineries" in the *Grand Traverse Herald*, February 18, 1859.

CHAPTER 14 • Life at the End of a Peninsula

"The Future of Traverse City," *Grand Traverse Herald*, April 8, 1869, 2.

"Grand Traverse Bay," *Grand Traverse Herald*, November 3, 1858, 2.

Leach, D. L., *A History of the Grand Traverse Region*, Traverse City, MI, *Grand Traverse Herald* Publishers, 1883.

Powers, Perry F., *A History of Northern Michigan and Its People*, Chicago: Lewis Publishing Company, 1912.

Chapter 15 • Say, Sis, Is the Doctor In?

Advertisement for Dr. Rosenthal, *Grand Traverse Herald*, 3, June, 1886.

Anonymous interview, heading: Rosenthal, Augusta Louise (Mrs. Isaac A. Thompson) transcription dated April 10, 1940, Bentley Historical Museum, Ann Arbor, MI.

"Death Came to Him Today," *Evening Record* (Traverse City, MI), 25 February, 1908, 1.

Isaac A. Thompson vs. Augusta Louise Rosenthal-Thompson, Grand Traverse Chancery Index, Case 1076, roll 28, p. 4223.

Keating, John William, M.D. ed., *The Physician and Surgeon: A Professional Medical Journal*, Jan. to Dec, 1906, Detroit and Ann Arbor, p. 191.

"Life and Times of the Lady Doctor," *Grand Rapids Herald*, Keith Strohpaul, 28 September, 1947, Feature Section, 1+.

Morantz-Sanchez, Regina, "The Female Student Has Arrived: The Rise of the Women's Medical Movement," in *Send Us a Lady Physician: Women Doctors in America, 1835-1920*, New York: W.W. Norton and Co. 1985, pp. 59-69.

Portrait and Biographical Record of Northern Michigan. Record Publishing Co., Chicago, 1895, p. 191.

Rosenthal-Thompson, Louise, "The Importance of Rectal Exploration in Children," *Journal of the State Medical Society*, 4, Jan-Dec, 1905. pp. 578-82.

Selmon, Bertha L., "History of Women in Medicine," *Medical Women's Journal*, October, 1948, pp. 58-52.